A LIFE WITH SPIRIT

June Barclay

with Love

June Barclay

June Barclay is a spiritual healer who lives in Devon and who works with Angels & her Guides to help heal others. Although she has always felt the presence of angels her spiritual journey really began after the passing of her son Stuart at the age of 20. This is the story of how she came to turn her grief at his loss into a way of helping others. The book is aimed at those who wish to explore a spiritual life and contains guidance and ideas to help along the journey.

A message from Uriel

Uriel brings peace and this wonderful golden glow. It's the glow of the sun to brighten your day. If there is anything you feel you need to be brave about you can rely on Uriel. She has put a golden glow over this book. The book has healing contained within its pages and so much love. The Angels are so happy that you have picked up this book and run with it.

Open your heart and realise the Angels are here for you and they bow down before you

A LIFE WITH SPIRIT

An introduction to leading a spiritual life through
conversations & channelled messages with
Angel Healers June Barclay and Stuart Barclay

Interviews by Jacqueline Wallace & June Grose
Edited by Marilu Wren

June Barclay
A Life with Spirit

ISBN 978-1-3999-0050-8

ISBN 978-1-3999-0050-8

9 781399 900508 >

Acknowledgments

All the interviewees in this book gave their time, love and their stories to create the narrative in section two. They told their whole story with courage and care and we listened and were grateful for their honesty. Once they became familiar with Spirit and the power of the Angels, they chose to use their knowledge for good. Their generosity has enabled the reader to understand that everyone has a different route to finding Spirit. This then is their gift to you all.

(Apart from Stuart and June all names have been changed)

Table of contents

PART THREE

A message from June

When I look back over my life I can see where Spirit stepped in and held me up, supported me, loved me and kept me on the path to become where I am now. I have always felt I had a path to walk and if and when I stepped off it Spirit really let me know. My life has always felt guided and as long as I do what Spirit plans it's ok. I have tried to test the water either side of the path but it has certainly not worked for me. You could say that it's not good, right or sensible to follow Spirit but I've always known for whatever reason this is me. I have my own idea of the ways things should happen and then I get a different version given to me. I cannot explain in enough words to show you all how every step of my life has led to me being the person, medium and healer I am today. I really believe there has been a plan to get me to be in Devon with the people I have in my life right now and to write this book.

As I sit here, I see the path I have walked behind me. It was never straight, I veered and pushed against life until I was ready to sit and listen to my own loving guidance. Believe me I have been to hell and back again and at one time all I had was the strength of the Spirit world to support me. I know now all the people I have met along the way family, friends and acquaintances have been my biggest teachers, even the ones that walked away in my darkest moments, I would like to thank them all. That is what made me move away from Essex and find the most wonderful friends and a beautiful place. I live here in Devon with my husband and soulmate and I believe this the nearest thing to heaven that you can get on earth.

Preface

Following a Spiritual life comes in many forms. We might choose from the various religions gaining comfort from their doctrines and enjoying their festivals because we feel they provide structure to our lives and a sense of community. Equally there are those who reject the concept of organised religion, feeling that interpretations of the major texts, the Bible, the Koran, the Torah etc., have become either diluted or too proscriptive. Once we take a certain path as the only path, once we believe we are right and others are wrong, once we are determined that everyone should believe what we believe then our humanity and compassion can only take a back seat.

Love and compassion for ourselves and others are the central foundations of all religions. For example, the Christian Bible encourages us to 'do unto others as we would like done unto us' (Luke 6:31); in Buddhism it is said that compassion for all sentient beings is the true road to living a happy life. The reality is that all sentient beings are born, live and die and for some people that is sufficient information. Many others though feel there is more than this, some want to know more about the possibility of other realities other possibilities and ways of living that might stretch beyond death but also help us to live in a way that feels acutely aware of the beauty of the world and the potential of love.

Many religions teach and many Spiritual workers know that there are whole worlds and other realms that exist beyond this reality. They are given proof of it in their daily lives. These individuals tend to have taken time to sit and listen and to live mindfully. In taking time to calm their minds negative thoughts can vanish and a clear positive mind can be generated. Many religions call this prayer, others call it meditation but there is increasing evidence that it helps to reduce anxiety and increase wellbeing (Baer et al 2012). Sitting and thinking helps to develop intuition. From intuition we begin to hear and feel Spirit and through Spirit we can be guided to help ourselves and to help others.

In this book we have brought together a range of people from very different backgrounds to talk about their life with Spirit. Their common experience is that they have spent time with a remarkable woman called June. She is the central figure in the book, but the book is more about how she has created the effect of a pebble in water and the ripples don't stop moving. Those who have spent time with her feel they can go away and follow their own paths and explore their own minds and listen to their own voices. Some have used their experiences to support others and some have used their experiences to try to live as good a life as possible.

Another key figure in this book is Stuart, June's son. Stuart took his own life some years ago but since then has appeared to many of the people whose stories are written here. He works with June in her healing and supports others to do similar work. His story and how he uses his strengths now is another pebble that creates waves. Stuart creates waves and June creates the ripples which support people to live their best lives.

Learning from the experiences of others is often how we learn to navigate our own world. June uses her life-learning and contacts with the Spirit world to help many people to find their way. She is guided by Angels to work as a healer and leads regular meditation groups supporting people who come with problems or to seek answers. She is the centre around which those who work with her come to understand meaning in their lives and the potential problems that may be causing them to feel unhappy or unwell.

The book is not a biography although it contains some of June's life experiences. We have used these to explain how she came to 'see' the world differently and how she developed her 'seeing' skills and her relationships with the Angels to help others. She now wants to reach a wider audience so she has decided to write down her story and to reach out to those who are lost or in need of unconditional love.

June's story is also used to give context to the experiences provided by her and others, about how individuals work with the Spirit world to inform their behaviour and choices.

This is not a self-help book. The stories were all reported and transcribed and explain June's influence on the lives of the story tellers and how they developed their awareness of the Spirit world through her. If the stories help readers and support them as they explore further the potential Spiritual influences on their life choices then this will be an added bonus.

From the experiences described the readers will have to make up their own minds about how they might pay attention to the voices in their heads. They will learn to understand how their soul speaks to them. They can then be guided to both feel good about themselves and also to reject the negative thoughts/ego which so often spoil the experience of living.

"Wake up and smell the Roses"
Stuart Barclay

PART ONE

The next section provides an interview with June about her first contacts with the Spirit world and how those contacts began to shape her life.

June Barclay

JUNE: THE PROTECTION OF THE ANGELS

June settled quietly on her sofa and prepared for her interview first by checking in with her Spirit guides and then by carefully choosing some Angel cards (see later) to guide her. Once she felt ready to begin the interview she indicated she was happy to turn on the digital recorder. She spoke quietly and calmly and sometimes stopped to think deeply about what she wanted to say.

Q: Tell me about how you knew about Angels?

J: I never saw Angels as a child. I felt a presence. I felt protected. I felt I could do anything. As a really young child I used to walk about outside in the middle of the night. My friend lived at the end of the road and it was always dark. I was very young, maybe 5 years old, and I'd walk back in the dark to my house but I never felt frightened.

I never felt I really needed my parents because I had this bigger thing around me. I felt quite self-contained. I remember feeling one of the family but not of the family.

I knew things would happen before they would happen – intuition I suppose. I felt invincible as a kid.

Q: Did it frighten you?

J: No never. I would walk home from school and I would know if someone was visiting our house before I got there when I got home. I knew if I'd ordered something from a catalogue that it would be there. It was a real knowing. So, it started with the knowing.

Q: Did you have friends at school?

J: Yes, I had a friendship group and I used to go out, but I didn't need anybody. I didn't want boyfriends. One of my friends she moved out of town and I would visit her there but I always felt she needed me more than I needed her.

Q: Do you still feel the same way?

J: Yes, I like, I love, having friends but I don't feel I need them. Maybe it's because I've got Charlie (her husband) and he's been with me since I was 17 or maybe it's more but I don't feel I need anyone else although I do love having people around.

Q: How do you know if someone is significant in your life?

J: The other side of being in touch with the Spirit world is that they put things and people on your path and that was Charlie.

When I met Charlie I thought 'It's never going to work'. He just wasn't my type. However, there was pressure from my friends to make up a foursome with Charlie so, reluctantly, I went.

That first night Charlie picked me up from my friend's house in his flash car. As I was walking up the stairs in front of him I heard a really loud voice, a man's voice, I don't know whether it was an Angel, but he said, '*you're going to marry him*'. It was the first time I heard a voice.

Q: What does that mean 'you heard it?'

J: It was very loud and in my head and I was just incensed. I thought 'you're having a laugh!' I thought what's all this about? It was the first time I heard the words, any words.

Q: You weren't alarmed about hearing a strange man's voice in your head?

J: No, isn't that odd? It wasn't shock horror. That was all they said. Can you imagine, I was only 17! They might as well have told me I was going to fly to the moon!

Q: Did you believe the voice?

J: Yes totally, not that it made me marry him. The voice was all encompassing but I didn't look at Charlie from that moment on and think I am going to marry you. I just felt comfortable with it all. I heard that voice and didn't freak out. I don't know why I had to hear that voice that night.

Q: And before that time, you had never heard a voice before?

J: No and I didn't again. It didn't bother me. Then the night before I got married, I know they (the Spirits) were there again talking about the arrangements for the wedding. They talked about my Dad. He had a heart attack on the day we got married. The cars didn't arrive on time. I knew all this would happen. I was used to that knowing about things before they happened. No voices just the knowing. Because I think they sort of feed me the stuff beforehand so I can cope with it when it happens.

So, on my wedding day I was quite calm.

Q: So, there are two sides of you. One is the shy June who has some anxiety about herself and then this other confident June, supported by the Spirit world, who describes herself as 'invincible'?

J: Yes, I like observing but don't like putting myself forward but increasingly in my life I find I have to do that and when I do it's like something takes over to help me. If it wasn't about Spirit and just about me, I couldn't do it. Maybe that's something I've got to work on and get over it.

Q: So, on the one hand you are happy to have the Spirit talk through you and in public, you feel absolutely safe and secure in the knowledge they are there and will work through you....

J: Yes completely

... and then on the other hand there is June who is worried about her appearance and who she is and being the centre of attention. The two sides don't seem to have much to do with each other.

J: Yes I suppose that's it. For example at my 70th birthday party my friend asked me to give a speech and I was absolutely horrified. There is a photo of me with my hands in front of my face when they are singing happy birthday. But I did talk because they were the words of the Spirit.

Q: So, you have to trust that the Spirit world will help you and you won't be left high and dry as June alone facing an audience?

J: Yes, that's exactly it. When I started doing the work (healing and therapy) I didn't feel them there and I just had to trust that they were there. Then they were there with me and I could feel and see them. I always waited until I saw an Angel before I started work. Not so much now after all these years. Now I don't see or feel I just know when they have joined me and I'm working. When I'm in the therapy room now I sometimes ask them if they are there and they always are of course but while I'm working doing healing I'm not aware of their presence at all.

Q: So how long was it between hearing the first voice and knowing you had to pay attention to what was going on?

J: It wasn't like that. It was just the norm. I didn't hear voices as clear as that first time telling me to marry Charlie.

Q: Can you tell me how your awareness developed over time and maybe describe some of the things that happened to convince you of the presence of the Spirit world in your life?

J: I got married and my dad died the time my first son Darren was born. I really thought I'd see my dad because he was so into all this Spiritual stuff but I didn't. I was surprised. I didn't see him until the night I had my third son Carl. Then I saw my Dad and he'd been dead about 5 years then.

I had terrible deliveries for all three boys. With my third son it was Charlie's birthday the next day and I thought I'll go to bed and it will be a nice surprise the next day. Well, I woke up in the middle of the night. My waters broke and I had to go downstairs to the loo. I saw the reflection of Dad's glasses in the mirror and I knew he was there. I wondered why he was there. I went back upstairs and said to Charlie I think I'd better go to the hospital. That was the first night I saw my Dad. Then he never left.

Q: Why do you think it was Carl he came with and not the other two?

J: I don't know really other than Carl was a bloody nuisance! I never asked my Dad why he came then. He was everywhere. It doesn't matter where I was there was my Dad. When I was driving, I could see him in the rear-view mirror sitting on the back seat of the car large as life. I knew what he was wearing. I never thought to ask him what he was doing there.

Q: You just accepted it? Did you see him absolutely as clearly as I'm seeing you?

J: Absolutely clearly. I don't know why we didn't talk. I suppose if you haven't had that training to ask you just don't. I find that odd now that I didn't think to ask him. Maybe I thought you needed a third party (a Spiritualist) to ask but of course I know now you don't.

So, I continued to see my dad. Charlie thought I was going mad when I told him I saw my dad all the time. Then one night I saw my first Angel.

All the things you think an Angel looks like, it doesn't look like that at all. It was night-time and we were in bed. I felt a presence and I thought 'oh my God there's something really big in this room!'. What I saw was … if you can imagine a swan's neck, it was this long thin neck. Even to this day I can feel the feathers. It came over the bed. The feathers were short. I got up and put all the lights on in the house. I was really alarmed. Charlie got up early the next morning and he couldn't understand why all the lights were on. I just told him I'd seen my dad again.

Anyway, he went off to work as a lorry driver and later I got a phone call from his work asking where Charlie was. He hadn't turned up at the depot. Then I knew what had happened. Immediately I put the phone down it rang again, and it was Charlie and he said 'If you ever see your dad again at night I'm not going to work in the morning!'. His lorry had jack knifed down a ditch and he'd lost the windows and the top of the cabin. All his tools had scattered. He walked out without a scratch.

Q: So, you said you were quite happy with presences, but this seems to have frightened you?

J: I think if you go to bed and are generally worrying about everyday things, the children and what you must do, and you are woken suddenly by something unexplained it is reasonable to be scared. It's new and unknown.

Q: Was this like when you had premonitions as a young girl?

J: I think it was the next step up. I think that Angel was Charlie's Guardian Angel and it protected him from the catastrophic crash.

Q: Do you see Angels now?

J: I don't see Angels, I see colours. I know they are there. My nose itches. I sometimes feel really hot. I think there is someone new with me at the moment because my chin itches.

Q: So back then you were alarmed. Now you are more used to it?

J: Yes, it was just alarming in the middle of the night. I didn't talk about it much to anyone. I was so busy at that time of my life, I accepted there were presences around me but I didn't have time to concentrate on it. I couldn't talk to Charlie or his family they wouldn't have understood so I just carried on.

And June has carried on. She is supported in her work by her Angels and by her beloved son Stuart. In the next section the interview continued but this time we concentrated on the events that led up to Stuart taking his own life.

A LIFE CHANGING EVENT

It was difficult for June to talk about the loss of Stuart but she felt it was key to understanding how her life changed both in terms of her current experience and her work with Spirit.

Q: I want to ask you about what happened around the time your son Stuart died. Can you tell me about that?

J: When we moved to a new house I remember standing on the back steps. I did hear a voice that day and the voice said *'you are going to grow old in this house'*. I don't think he meant old age. I think he meant that the experiences in the house would age me. Even though I had all those kids and all that responsibility I was still quite young, in my early thirties. I thought about that after Stuart killed himself and realised that the voice had been telling me about difficulties ahead.

I knew the week before. He and his brother Carl had been in Bangkok and I don't know what happened there, but it was catastrophic. Stuart's brother had to bring him home and he was in a really bad way. I didn't see anything at that time, but the house started to move like in an earthquake. It's like I couldn't control what was going on. I would go out and when I came back the house still felt like it was moving. I felt like I was fighting what was going on in that house.

Q: Did you feel there were lots of presences in the house

J: Yes

Q: Were they there when you moved in, or had you bought them with you?

J: No, they arrived in the last week of Stuart's life. I knew it was bad and I knew he would die no matter what I did. The house was actually moving. I knew even if we took him to hospital or whichever doctor we saw it wouldn't change things.

On the morning Stuart died Charlie was taking him to the hospital. Stuart walked past Charlie as he was getting his coat on and went out to his gym that was in the garage. Charlie went out to find him but couldn't open the door to the gym. He had to break it down and that is where he found Stuart's body.

Q: So, it was premeditated?

J: Absolutely. He knew what he was doing. God took him. I've seen pictures of people who have killed themselves, but they always look anguished. Stuart looked completely at peace as though he was only sleeping. He looked twelve again. Even the undertaker remarked on it. She would sit with him in the Chapel of Rest because she felt he had such a peaceful presence. I knew then that God needed him more than I did and this was how it was to be.

My friend drove over the next day to sit with me. We were in the conservatory. I suddenly realised the house had stopped moving. There was a complete peace. A peace I've never felt before. That day they showed me how he was being taken to heaven. I saw him clearly in a bubble talking to someone. I don't know who. He had on a green jacket and his hair was curly as usual. He was smiling and happy. I watched the bubble start on the floor and it went up and disappeared through the roof. I thought 'they're taking him home'. The peace was lovely. How I could have such peace after what had happened the previous day I don't know.

Q: How were you feeling?

J: I just knew then that although it was so sad that I would have a coping mechanism.

Q: How do you make sense of it all now?

J: In a way, it sounds peculiar, but I feel very privileged.

Q: In some ways are you saying Stuart has given you the life you have now. Is that right?

J: Yes. He was in the house a lot afterwards. I sensed him at the funeral. I knew he was there. He loved his food. He would forever be in the kitchen. We had one of those combi microwaves. For days after he passed over we would go in the kitchen and the microwave would be on. The knobs would spin and the dials would turn. I had to physically go into the kitchen and say to him 'can you stop it now you're disturbing us!'. That went on for ages. I had a friend who we would visit sometimes and she would say 'I knew you were coming, I've had that little sod here all morning turning my microwave on'. She wasn't a Spiritual person, but she knew it was him.

Q: So, Stuart would turn up before you did at a friend's house? Why do you think he did that?

J: I think it was just a connection. I don't think he did it to frighten anyone. I think he had found a new way of being and he was going to let us know all about it.

Q: Do you think he was at peace?

J: I don't know about that. I felt at peace. I never questioned that he was around.

Q: This is a difficult question but many people would say you were so distressed by losing your son that you have developed the work you have done since as a way of trying to keep some connection. A psychological response rather than something Spiritual. What is it about the work you've done since that has proved to you that it's not a response to loss created by yourself?

J: When it happened, I had this real urge to go looking to find answers to what had happened. That's a normal psychological response. I tried various things. I'd never meditated with anybody. I didn't really know anything about it. Now I do believe you are guided to people who can help you. There was a lady I was introduced to and I was guided to go and talk to her. I just felt very strongly when her name was mentioned that I needed to see her. She said on the strength of meeting you I feel guided to run a meditation group. She obviously felt some connection with me too.

I continued to go to the new meditation group. I had a friend whose sister was very Spiritual. She used to see people. My friend said would I take her sister to the new mediation group too. We agreed to share lifts. One evening when she turned up to come with me, she said

'Are we not using your car tonight then?'

'Yes, I said, of course we are'

'Well what's that young boy doing sitting in the driving seat of your car then?'

'What does he look like?' I said, and she described him exactly. She had never come into my house before and she had never seen any pictures of Stuart.

13

'I think you better come in' I said, 'There's something I need to explain.

I showed her the photo of Stuart and told her what had happened.

'No, He's sitting out there in the car!'

I said 'I know, because he is coming with us'

So, as I said he led the way for me to do the healing work I'm doing now. I did not expect it to happen.

Q: So, the initial response was 'why me?' and a normal psychological searching but the end point was to bring to the fore something you had been working with on and off all your life?

J: Yes, I had the Spiritual side of my life there all the time since I was small but Charlie and me and the kids had a good life so I didn't have time to focus on it. The children wanted for nothing. I could say, 'why my kid?' but the truth is it had to happen that way for me to finally take notice of the Spiritual influences on my life and to then decide what to do with them.

Q: So, it doesn't really matter whether your present work was a psychological reaction and/or the trigger for the development of your Spiritual life. You always seem to have had a knowing and an awareness of atmospheres and beings. It almost appears that your tragedy led you to be much more aware of other people's pain having been rendered so vulnerable yourself. Since Stuart passing over you have been able to help so many people and that has been a valuable result of your sadness.

J: When I first moved to Devon after Stuart had passed over, I went to another meditation group, just for me. I just wanted to sit quietly in the corner and meditate. Then the leader of that group said 'I need to talk to you'. She said:

'You think everyone is like you. You really don't know what you have.'

'I don't know what you're talking about' I said. I had never told anyone much about what I thought and experienced. In the time I grew up you would have been locked up for saying the sort of things I experienced so I just didn't. I had lived a busy life and the 'knowing' side was just one part of it.

Q: Why did you choose meditation as a way of trying to find answers?

J: Well at first I went to a meditation group because the leader was a Spiritualist and I wanted answers. So, it was her who decided on meditation for me.

Q: And you liked it?

J: I loved it. It was a way of finding peace when the world had gone mad. I could cut off from the pain in my life. I just could go and be in my own little space. At that time I was consumed by grief so I didn't question why my new acquaintance had started a mediation group. I was aware she was very very kind and I felt safe meditating in my own little space. Charlie and I couldn't talk about it because it brought the horror back for him. I had somewhere to go where I felt cared for. It felt like I'd had my arms and legs cut off and the meditating helped me to just be quiet.

Q: So, it helped with a search for peace in your own self?

J: Yes, I was searching and looking...

Q: So, people you met said they wanted to work with you. Were you open to that?

J: Oh yes. Everyone was falling apart and the only strength I got was from going and sitting in that group. I had to be strong for the family. I had other children to look after. We had to go on. The meditation group was a life saver.

Then I joined a healing group and I got healing and that really helped. I wanted to be a medium actually and I went for training several times but at each attempt I got unwell. The group leaders kept saying you're not a medium you are a healer. I wanted to be a medium because I like giving the messages.

Q: Have the people you worked with talked to you about Stuart?

J: Yes. I worked with someone. I'd known her for years and then she said 'I want to talk to you about Stuart'. 'He was an Ascended Master. To me he was just my son but hearing that really helped and I realised how blessed I had been that he had chosen me as his mother. She said he hadn't had many lives but in one he was St Bernadette, the Nun who created Lourdes in France. I didn't know about any of these people. I had to learn it all. I did realise that day though that the voice that told me to marry Charlie was the voice that led all this to happen and if I hadn't married Charlie then maybe Stuart would not have been born and lost and that there was now a clear purpose to it all. I am privileged to have been given a gift.

Q: But also that he continues to work through you?

J: Yes. In addition to his help with the healing work he has proved himself useful in other ways. For example, Mary is a friend who lives next door. She had two sons Peter and Mark. They both became paratroopers. Peter went to Afghanistan. Whilst he was away Mary wanted to re-decorate his room and decided she would put a border around the top of the wall. Mary and I went to the local building suppliers but all the borders were pink. I was suddenly conscious of Stuart being there and he said 'I *think you should try that top basket on top of the cabinet'.* I said to Mary that if she could reach the high basket she would find what she wanted. Mary looked and there was the border she had been looking for. It had black Japanese writing around the edge and was a lovely blue. There was only one roll she bought it hoping it would be enough. Mary phoned me later and said the border had been exactly the right length.

When Peter returned from his tour of duty he was amazed by the border. He questioned his mum about how she had known about the Japanese writing. He had had exactly the same letters tattooed on his arm.

Q: So, going forward what happened when you came to Devon?

J: Well I went to a Spiritualist for one-on-one meditation. Then one day the Spiritualist she said well I'm pregnant so I'm handing my meditation group over to you. I said no I couldn't but then I went home and asked Charlie if he minded us using the living room as a meditation room once a week and he didn't so that was settled! He even joined in.

At first, I felt it was just like having friends over but I did ask the Angels for help. I felt completely comfortable with it because they helped me do it. It just felt natural and they were speaking through me because I couldn't make the stuff up - I didn't know it.

That was nine years ago. The group has got so big I've had to build a healing hut in the garden so Charlie could have the living room back.

In the next section Stuart was asked to make his contribution to the book.

STUART'S STORY

S tuart has made his presence clear to many of the members of the group June works with and using a dowsing crystal (see later) indicated that he wanted to be part of this book. Through most of the interview June was in deep meditation. The interview, as did all interviews in this book concerning June, took place in June's living room, a sunny bright room in a house by the sea in Devon. Through her windows there are wonderful views of June's healing room in her garden full of roses and then beyond that the coastline. The view outside can change from moment to moment depending on the weather. On sunny days you can see to the horizon and on misty days you can barely see the garden. Her living room remains quiet and peaceful no matter what is going on outside its four walls. She sits quietly, hands in her lap, eyes closed and asks the Angels for help. A short time passes before she begins to speak. The words and phrasing are so different from her usual pattern of speech. She dips in and out of her channelling but sometimes during the session she would turn to the interviewer with a special message from the Angels particularly for her. Most times June has very little memory of what was said and is sometimes surprised when she reads the transcript of the interviews.

Stuart: from the Spirit world speaking to and through June.

Although I work with the Archangels I am learning and finding out how to use my energy and I know you know it's powerful. I do watch and I do come to be with you as that link is always there and I am so grateful, even though you never asked me to leave you, because it has allowed me to do this work. I am so sorry for the sadness I have brought. It was never meant to hurt you, it was for your growth, for you to understand that the Spirit world is never far away and you as humans are always connected. I can only tell you it was my time and I was needed here. We can do far more from behind the veil than you can on earth. I know Mum you do have the Spirit world to come and speak to people and this is as you know a different energy from working with the Angels. The Angels speak through you and the Spirit world lets you speak to them and they speak back to you. I know you know the difference.

Sometimes it's my job to bring a person/Spirit through to visit you. I always know when there is a young person that is coming to you to listen. I am always there standing next to you because I know you know the pain so many young people feel. I know that this is difficult. I have always had to work with young people like a Samaritan to stop them taking their own lives. That is part of my job.

I know it's hard for you to understand but I can be with you and I can be in another place. I can be in lots of places at once. I am far happier doing my work here. There is always a sense of achievement when I know I have done my job well and somebody feels the healing. I know what you do and I know that you care. Please don't be sad because I'm always here. I would like you to know that I worked with Raphael to deliver the healing that was so important to me and to you.

Stuart then added some words on the experience of grief and grieving. He says he feels strongly that the human race grieves too long and there needs to be some explanation about why this is not necessarily helpful to those left behind. He believes grieving is natural for a length of time but then it becomes counterproductive.

Grieving changes everyone and will do forever but maybe we should rejoice the change. The key thing is he said you are a breath away. You have to let your loved ones go. You have to practice this. It isn't easy. It takes so much practice.

It's about the human race, about death the way you perceive it - the outpouring of grief. We need to let people know that those who pass on move on and change the same way that you change. There is an evolution that goes on far beyond what you can comprehend. People need to know that we go on and that we don't die. Our energy is always with you. We are just a breath away and we find it sad that people grieve for so long. I know that my mum has grieved and I know she misses me, but I am just a word away and my energy will always be around. It's hard for us to understand why people grieve for so long. We see from here that they damage themselves by grieving and they need words of wisdom to change that.

I understand that you have to grieve for the loss of the physical body. Think about it this way, my mum's children do not live with her now but she still senses their energy. It's the same with me. I would not be living with her now but I'm with her more than I

21

would have been. I say sorry a lot to her for what I did but it was my time and I had other things to do. I can be in more places than one as you have noticed. Relatives and close friends to somebody that dies need to understand that it's not their fault, it's just the way the human body breaks down and we come home.

The energy is vast and more available to people because we are here. We grow and change like you grow and change. We do have jobs to do and callings the same as you. People who live with grief are not living their lives. Grief changes the energy in their body. There is no sticking plaster to change what happened.

Before you come back to live on the earth plain, you decide the things that will change for you on the next journey to make you move spiritually and to change your energy. It is all decided before you come back to live here. It brings us sadness that people do not understand. If only they knew it's grief that is killing them. I feel strongly about this. The grief causes black deposits in the body and all their wanting and wishing will not change what has happened.

The human race needs to understand this to stop some of the pain and the unhappiness. If they could only understand their journey is preordained before they come into the world and grasp that things are meant to be and there is no blame and nobody is to blame. We need people to know the truth. When people have grieved for too long, they look back and realise they did have a life and they have wasted their lives by grieving. Life on earth is precious. You have free will. You have the ability to love each other if only people would stop putting a wall around themselves to prevent them feeling this love. We all come from the same place, we are a spark of life and you are all in it together.

My last words it's time for humanity to wake up and smell the roses!

June had a break after delivering her son's story. So we resumed the interviews some time later and discussed all the Angels who help her in her work.

ANGELS AND THE SPIRIT WORLD

J une thought it might be useful to define what is meant by Angels and Spirits. The Angels presented here are the primary ones who work with her regularly, there are many others. As usual she settled herself in her living room and went into a channelled quietness. The words delivered through her from the Angels are in italics.

J: The Archangels are God's messengers. They all come with a different vocation. They are the source that is sent from God. They also work as one.

We bring the light to light the way forward for those who call on us. It's love that brings them to earth. We work in the name of love and exactly like Guardian Angels (see later) *we can only help when we are asked to help. We are here with you but we are also everywhere.*

J: They have shown me the universe and I see they fill the universe. It's almost like they have this protective shield over the universe.

Everyone can ask for healing or comfort or strength. We can come and help you to feel those things, but free will is your choice. Most people in the universe can feel lonely because they don't know how to ask but anyone can just ask and we will come.

Describing her experience of meeting the Angels June said:

When Stuart died I really did cry out for help but even before that they were around a lot telling me I had a job to do. Part of my job now is this book.

They say that we are standing on the edge of a precipice and have to step off now. They describe this time for humanity as 'being in the shadows' but there are more and more people actively listening for Angel voices and this gives them strength. They describe it as '*the veil is thinner between our world and the Spirit world*' so they can now be more accessible.

For too long people have concentrated on money and possessions and yet at the same time feeling desperate for help. That's why the Angels want to be around more to help because they feel people have lost their way. We need to call them back to our hearts and ask for their help. It's not enough now for me to just sit in my healing room and talk to a few people. The Angels call it an '*epidemic of lack*'.

The idea is not to make people rush to church to find answers because some people haven't found sustenance in religion. There are many paths to God. A church community may provide security for some, but it is not necessary to go to church in order to feel the love of God and the Angels. Many religions talk about love, but the message is so often lost in the interpretation of the texts on which those religions are based. Spending time listening to the voices of the Angels is not based on a text so the channels to the Angels are about pure love. They need no interpretation because everyone can hear them first-hand. They just need to learn to listen. This is about love and caring. It's not about being down on your knees and praying, it's just about asking for help and hearing answers and there is no need for the trappings of religion to be able to listen.

We are not expecting anything back we just want to uplift people and help them feel love in their heart. There is no demand to do more than ask for help. Church can make you feel you are owned. That is religion, it's not what this is about. God is all loving and caring. There is no hell. There is no punishment. There is definitely no brimstone and fire. This is not fear based. This is pure unadulterated love from the source, and we are his messengers

June then went on to describe some of the Angels she works with. She was channelling their words and they are reported here verbatim.

Archangel Michael

J: Can I talk to Archangel Michael. He holds the sword of truth. For me he comes on a blue ray which helps me communicate with him.

I come with the strength to help you fight your battles. I give you the courage if you are willing to seek and ask me. I will give you the courage to speak your truth. As a member of the human race you have connections to each other which are formed from the solar plexus. These can be good connections, or they can be attachments that interfere with your journey. If you ask for my help to sever those attachments that is part of my job. I want to help you in negative situations.

J: I ask him if I feel somebody needs his support and it's like two arms are there to hold the person up and to reassure them. He has just told me people can call on him during meditation. He is showing me a path, the path we walk and our paths generally can get overgrown with brambles and weeds and we can get stuck. He can clear all that. He says call me a gardener! He can make the path easier.

Raphael

J: Raphael is the healer. He works with me when I'm doing the healing. I step out of my body and he moves in. He knows where to put my hands.

I come on the emerald green path and I work with June by standing behind her. Energy filters through the crown chakra. I am the Angel of love. My heart sinks when your heart sinks.

J: Raphael and Michael are both telling me they don't want to be put on a pedestal. This is the part they play, and we are all equal. In fact they bow to us for coming back to earth to try to change things. They say they are our support system in the work we do.

If you would like to think of it that we are your life, your blood, then that is how close we are to you. There is no word in language that can give you an understanding of the love that we feel for you. June feels that love when she does healing. We stand here in reverence to you, watching over you from an outer world. I bring you joy I bring you happiness and I bring you healing. These are my words to you.

Uriel

I come to June as a gold light and I bring hopes and dreams. We know you have wishes and desires and when you have the right wish and desire for your life you feel an energy that comes with it and I bring that energy. I wish to shine a gold light on your hopes and dreams. I come with a ray of sunshine and lift you up. I come when there is emotional distress. Emotional distress can bring physical illness, so my wish is you ask for help before physical disease arrives from the emotional hurt.

Although you think of us as three (Michael, Raphael and Uriel) *we work as one when we are healing through June. It is the reason when you give healing June you do not have to know the nature of the disease or emotional problem. You just have to open your heart and mind and allow us to do the work. You allow us to give you the words and use the words and may I say there is a certain amount of trust that has to be applied.*

Gabriel

J: For me Gabriel comes on a white ray. He is here in front of me and he is a shaft of white light. He comes blowing a trumpet and when he blows it I know all will be well and things will turn out for the best. He comes with energy of good deeds and happiness, almost like promises that you have asked for and he clears the way for good news to come. His desire is to make the human race joyous. He just told me I am the singer. *If I could lift everyone out of their dark place, then my work has been done.* He doesn't come every time I work, only when the client feels ready to open their hearts and allow acceptance. When that happens he brings a wonderful joy and then things can change. He says there are stages people have to go through to get to this place mentally, physically and emotionally everything has to catch up with one another. *We want to show the world it can be a better place.*

Sandalphon

J: Sandalphon stands with me and is my Guardian Angel. His colour is a deep gold. He has been with me since the day I was born. He is one of the Angels that has lived on earth. He is Metatron's brother. He knows the pitfalls and unhappiness of everyday life. Sandalphon overlooks the work that I do, the meditation, the cards and the healing. He helps me organise and encourages me so that I know this is the way things are meant to be. He tries really hard to steer me on the right path. He finds me very frustrating because I don't always listen!

'June I place the right people on your path to help with the projects that we know that you learn from and I have had to help you to open your heart to those projects. I am your friend. I am your comforter in bad times, and I will always be standing here ready to help. I am the lover of music when you play music in your sessions. If you like I am the frivolous one who likes the candles and the music and the crystals. I come on that energy from the crystals and my love is never ending.

Time for yourself

There are many other Angels. Some of their names are mentioned in the Glossary. If you are interested in finding some connection with the Spirit world then take some time to find a comfortable place you like. Spend some time on your own. Breathe deeply and sit quietly. Initially your head will be full of all the worrries and thoughts about the 'should dos' in your life. Take five minutes out every day to do this. You can use the alarm on your phone or an alarm clock to tell you when the five minutes is up. That will stop you from checking constantly during the session and becoming distracted.

Over time being quiet will become easier and then, when your mind is quiet you can begin to ask questions from your Guardian Angel. This Angel has been with you since you were born and is waiting for you to listen. Don't worry if nothing comes to you initially. It's all about taking time.

PART TWO

In this next section there are answers to questions you might want answers to and extra material to help you on your path.

June Barclay

STARTING YOUR SPIRITUAL JOURNEY

More and more people are becoming interested in finding a Spiritual connection and an alternative to organised religion. Starting out can be very confusing. There are so many self-help books and guidance but it seems a minefield of 'experts' and it's difficult to know how to proceed. How do you go about finding the right person to guide you and how can you be assured you are getting advice that will help you in your search for answers? June asked the Angels to help her. Uriel came through:

We join you today and we have been listening to your discussions and are aware of your needs. We need to talk about how to find the right person for you to help with healing or Spiritual help. What you seem to forget is that you have a Guardian Angel that walks with you and the Guardian Angel knows exactly who you need to help you. The problem is most people do not know they have Guardian Angels and how much they can help. Most humans feel they are alone on planet Earth and they do not believe there is an outer guidance system for them to tap into. Sometimes it takes a tragedy or a life altering event they need help with and when they call for help it comes. When there are times of stress the Guardian Angel steps closer and offers a support system. I know June used to read a poem called footprints which talks about the experience of calling out and feeling you are lifted up and cared for by an outer calm. This is your Guardian Angel making him/herself felt.

Most times to find the right person you need to listen to the guidance you get from your Guardian Angel. It is a subtle energy that goes from your Angel to you. Unless you are used to listening you can miss it. Most people cry out for help at their worst times. It seems humans have to fall on their knees with distress to finally hear us. But, my dear ones, if you do it now you will be ready to receive help in times of need and you will hear us. Some people arrive knowing there are Angels guiding them and some will learn. Others may never know in this life.

The energy experienced is sometimes called God and that is fine but you all have God in your heart. Whether individuals wish to believe it or not we are all joined together with God's energy. The evolution for each person is different. Tapping into guidance has to be done freely because freewill is what humans have been given on earth. We cannot step in until we are called. We whisper in your ear, we engage with your solar plexus and you come to know you are on the right path.

We often come in dreams because your minds are at rest then. During the day you are so engaged with everyday activities that the path to listening is blocked. We offer signposts to all but you have to notice and be listening to realise the signs are directed at you. Older people have more time to listen and they understand a bit more as they have lived longer. They often begin to take notice of the signs and signals.

If you ask for guidance before you go to sleep we can move in overnight. So often having slept on your worry you wake up with the answer to your problems because we have been able to work with you as you slept. We are patient and we are loving and we understand the barriers you put up because you do not believe we are near. There is something missing in people, because you are so materialistic you lose the connection to Spirit. Sometimes we wish you could hear us and ask for help because you struggle so much but we wait to be called. Tragedy opens the door to thinking there might be something bigger. We are sad it so often has to be this way. Once called on we can show you the path to the person who can help on earth, the healer, the oracle card reader. Once you have had help you can begin to connect to your consciousness and hear the messages yourself.

Try meditation. You don't have to join a group although that can be very helpful starting off. Just sitting quietly and listening to your breath can quieten your mind in the first instance. Over time you will begin to hear the guidance given to you by your Guardian Angel. We know once you find the Spiritual path you feel the joy of connection and the answers you search for. You have someone to talk through your problems with and support you. We are your servants and we are so pleased to do this.

Footprints in the Sand by Mary Stevenson

One night I dreamed I was walking along the beach with the Lord.
Many scenes from my life flashed across the sky.
In each scene I noticed footprints in the sand.

Sometimes there were two sets of footprints,
other times there were one set of footprints.
This bothered me because I noticed
that during the low periods of my life,
when I was suffering from
anguish, sorrow or defeat,
I could see only one set of footprints.
So I said to the Lord,
"You promised me Lord,
that if I followed you,
you would walk with me always.
But I have noticed that during
the most trying periods of my life
there have only been one
set of footprints in the sand.
Why, when I needed you most,
you have not been there for me?"
The Lord replied,
"The times when you have
seen only one set of footprints,
is when I carried you."

During a different channeling session the Angels explained to June that when we are at our lowest ebb they are allowed to step in and hold us up, supporting us emotionally under the arms so we don't collapse;

"We bring in the light to support your darkness. When you are at your lowest ebb you give us permission to support you in that

way, to give you the emotional wellbeing to pick yourself and start over again. It's an inside job. We try to make you feel better about yourself, so we send the light to the dark to support you. This is a very human thing when you fall by the wayside, we just have to be there to steer you back on the path for you to be here for your soul lessons".

We discussed the timings of having prayers answered, how as human we are linear and as the Angels don't work that way we have to be patient. As an example, June talked about her son Carl, who has been out of her life since Stuart died, as he struggled to cope with losing his brother. For years June sent healing and asked for him back, only to be told that it didn't work with Carl's timing and that she would have to wait for him to return in his own time. June was reminded by the Angels *"that everyone is in their own Divine Timing. We can show you a clock with times on there, but the soul has to be ready to show up on that timing. It's the soul that has the clock".* They showed June a box that opened when it's time, to clarify the analogy of Divine Timing and how Carl was the perfect example of that.

We talk about how often when you are on your knees, begging for things to change, to be that low that you are open to hearing and know that things have to be different. That at times we have to be powerless in order for the shifts to happen in our lives once we have surrendered to Source

June confirms how the poem "Footprints" accurately portrays how it was for her after Stuart died, how she felt so propped up and supported by God through her darkest hours. She shared about the pain of grief and how you respond to it and how thanks to that poem she had the strength to continue.

The advice given here is helpful in that it mirrors many of the basic principles of both organised religion and the self-help books you see in bookshops. Trusting in yourself to find answers by spending some quiet time every day, settling your mind and learning to listen for guidance and clues, can really be the first steps to a Spiritual connection. It doesn't take lots of money. You don't necessarily have to buy help. Sometimes attending a few meditation sessions to start you off can be helpful. Sometimes visiting a healer can be illuminating. The guidance here tells us to practice taking time out, to be peaceful and quiet to trust that you have a Guardian Angel who is waiting to be called upon.

How will I know when I am making a connection?

June says it's different for everyone but most people say they get a sensation in their heart or solar plexus.

'It's like a peace that comes over me. Then I have to feel trust. They are always saying 'welcome' but I have to trust in the fact that they are there every time I talk to them. Even after all these years the delay is mine. I just have to keep making sure they are there. When I feel connected I repeat the word welcome to the group or person I am working with and then all the other things they intend to say seem to come without my help.

I don't see them in person I see colours, today it's gold and purple. I hear the words in my head but the sound appears to come with the colours.

At the end of the session it takes a long while to come to. If Charlie comes in and asks what I want for dinner or something it's like he is speaking a foreign language. It's like they are so close they take up all the available place in my head.

Sometimes several Angels will be around. I hear what I'm being told by one Angel and then I feel a different energy and it might be Stuart or another Angel. Then they will have something to say and I just pass it on.

I like the sense of peace and that their energy is uplifting. It's never bothered me, I'm not frightened. The only thing that bothers me is have I got the message right? Is it me or is it them? You say I am so articulate when I am channeling the Angels. so it's definitely not me because I am absolutely not that articulate in real life. I have done loads of workshops in front of people with their help. I feel very comfortable with what they say I should pass on but if I had to think of something to say to a large group of people on my own I'd be terrified. I think it's important that I continue to demand of myself that I trust in what is happening and that I question whether what I am saying comes from them or me. I am concerned if I became complacent or I didn't really make the connection that I could cause harm. It's like a damage limitation thing to make sure I say what they want me to say and not what I think should be said. I keep checking and will always do so.'

MEDITATION

June describes meditation as 'listening' and praying as 'asking'. The following description was delivered from the Angels working with June;

Everyone has a soul and when you meditate you touch your soul. There is a connection between being human and Spirit and soul. Every human has to come back multiple times to find the job they are meant to achieve. Meditation involves slow breathing and a connection to the earth. The slow breathing reduces the blood pressure and creates a state of wellbeing. Then the soul speaks loudest, sometimes in words and sometimes in pictures and sometimes in feelings.

If the soul doesn't learn lessons in one life you return again so meditation is really a good way to find out the specific reason you are here. If you spend time meditating, you know you are not alone. We are all born with Guardian Angels and the closer you can get to your Guardian Angels the more likely it is you can have a conversation with them and achieve your life goals. Guardian Angels aren't allowed to help until they are asked.

You all come with freewill but when things get tough you can feel supported by our Guardian Angels even if you don't believe in

God. We walk beside you throughout your life whether you know it or not. You are a spark of light from the universe.

If you are brave enough to accept the challenge a whole new world can open up. You meditate to exist in a moment and experience the eternal unconditional love of the Angels. You can get your own answers to questions you don't understand about your life. You have no need of help from elsewhere. If only you know how connected you are to the Spirit world. It's where you can receive support and love. Life is not easy. Everyday life is not the main reason you are here. Each of us has a task to fulfil and you will understand more of what that task is by working with the Spirit guides that have been with you from birth. You will feel their presence if you step into that meditative space.

My dear ones we say this with all the love from the Spirit world. If you reach out across the void we will be there to support you and make your journey easier.

June then went on to answer some questions:

Q: What can I do when I sit and breathe and all I can think about is everyday things?

J: Practice, attend a group and learn from others, buy CD's or look at films on YouTube (see Appendix).

Everything starts with the breath and working in a meditation group means your practice is guided and you can discuss what is happening.

Q: How often should I meditate for?

J: Start with every day for 15 minutes. Just sit quietly and concentrate on where you feel the breath coming in and out of your body. Don't worry if your thoughts wander. Just check them and go back to the breath. It doesn't matter if this happens 100 times. Don't try too hard. You are perfect just as you are. Just go back to the breath and start again. You can count the breath in groups of 10 if that helps. Some days you may not get past 3 before your mind wanders. It doesn't matter just start again.

During the day you might just stop what you are doing and concentrate on your breath, doing the washing up, taking a shower, walking or standing at the bus stop just be present in the moment with your breath. It won't change overnight. It might take years but eventually you will feel increasingly peaceful.

You will get more practiced at sitting quietly each day and taking some time to be peaceful. It can feel like daydreaming. Staring into space, taking some time to breathe quietly can be really useful. Just think to yourself 'I will daydream for a bit.' Be quiet with your thoughts. Don't get stuck on one particular thought just still your mind and relax.

June runs a regular mediation group called The Temple Path and some of her members describe her meditations as "a lovely way to relax and take time for yourself, it gives you a feeling of absolute calmness." And they "offer you a space where it is still possible to cultivate a conscious and real sense of connection with yourself and others, a much-needed medicine in these disorientating and dismantling times."

It's been pointed out that June's meditations are very healing "June's healing comes through in a deep way of which has saved me on many occasions, always appearing when I needed her most". and others "feel warm, soothing, familiar hug... I deeply relax when working with June and find I am taken away from myself and my body into a beautiful feeling of expanse and calm. When I come out .. I feel a strong sense of peace and deep nourishment. I know that I have received the healing that I needed at that time and I sense that the Angels were with me"

There's no doubt that the work the Angels do through June's mediation are very powerful and healing as another member commented "I have found since doing the meditation regularly with June, that I go much deeper and that my body receives healing that often shows itself the following day. The work that is done with the Angelic Realm is profound".

A Meditation on Love

June asked the Angels whether there was a meditation that might be useful to add to the book. Their first response was 'Lots!'

Dear friends let's talk about what holds people back from their experience of Spirit. You find it so hard to believe because you feel you are using your imagination, making it up. You feel you are inventing everything for your own benefit. It's so hard to grow and to be everything you want to be when you doubt the messages we send you. Imagination is a wonderful thing, it's like daydreaming, it's creates a place you can go and connect to the higher consciousness. Ask for your biggest and best ideas to come to fruition. Once you ask for help and let your heart open you can achieve anything.

The following is a guided meditation you can do on your own. It will help you to know you are not alone and help you to experience the unconditional love of the Angels.

First find a comfortable quiet place to sit where you will not be disturbed. Make yourself comfortable on a chair as this meditation suggests or lie on the floor or a bed. Make sure you will be warm enough so you might like a blanket over you.

'With your feet flat on the floor (or imagine your feet on the floor*) and your spine leaning on the back of the chair or bed take some nice deep breaths. Expand your stomach as you breathe in and let it rest when you breathe out. You will find lots of thoughts rushing through your mind. They don't matter just let them pass. Concentrate on the positive and leave the negative behind. Let go*

of the day. Another nice deep breath. Now just let your breath return to normal. Be aware of how the breath passes in and out through the end of your nose or allows your chest to rise slowly. You can count your breaths as you settle to help keep your mind focused. Count ten breaths in and out and then start again. If you lose track just gently start again.

Use your imagination. Think about the soles of your feet. From each foot there is a root. It can be of any size. Imagine your own roots. imagine the roots are going down to the centre of the earth. Take them down through the building down through the earth's core. Follow them in your mind's eye watch them go. Don't force it just watch them navigate the rocks and the waterways through tunnels and open spaces. Imagine the colours of the way as you pass through it. Finally bring your roots to the centre of the earth. It's a huge open area maybe with beautiful walls and shimmering light. In the centre of the open area there is a crystal just for you. It can be any shape, any size and any colour. Focus on the colour. Let this lovely colour wrap around the crystal. Feel its loving energy and allow that energy light to flow right up through the roots. Follow the roots all the way back to the soles of your feet. Take your time and continue to breathe gently.

Your body is made up of energy, of stars and of crystals. This energy will not hurt you, it's here to help support you. Take your crystal's energy, its light, into your body. Watch it travel through the soles of your feet and into your ankles. Feel the wonderful sense of letting go. It travels to your knees, your thighs, just let go and let the energy travel through you. Let it travel through the base chakra, up to the heart, the throat and to the third eye, to the top of your head, the crown centre. Let the wonderful light energy leave your crown and travel to the heavens. This is our higher consciousness where the Spirits and the Angels are waiting for you. Rest with them for a pure moment of peace.

Now bring that energy back through the crown centre, and the third eye. Let your eyes relax, let your throat chakra relax, your jaw drops and you relax. Take the crystal light across your shoulders and down your arms to your fingertips. Let your shoulders drop and release all the stress you hold there. Come back and down to the heart and release the tension around the rib cage, the lungs. Feel in your own space. Breathe.

Now to the solar plexus, our thinking centre where we feel vibrations of energy. Ask for it to be cleared. Now down to the sacrum, the centre of creativity. Down to the base of your body and the sexual organs. Just let go of the stress and channel the energy back down through the soles of your feet to the centre of the earth. Now you are connected to the centre of the earth and to the heavens.

You are now completely surrounded by protection. All your problems and stresses are released and you are at peace. From this place of quiet we can go to the inner heart. Take your imagination to the heart, the heart chakra centre. Imagine a rose there that is closed. Choose a rose of any colour you want. Imagine the rose opening to full bloom.

Move forwards to the centre of the rose. There is a door there. What colour is the door? What does it look like? Open the door. It opens to your inner temple. Open the door and step inside. This is where your soul resides. This is the place where you can experience the wonderful person that you truly are. The person who came back to earth to live a life. Life doesn't necessarily need to be perfect. Human beings are not always perfect but are always lovely.

Love yourself the way we love you. In the inner temple you will find a comfortable chair to sit on. Sit in it and wrap yourself in the love that is there for you. You are so loved. We wish you would stop berating yourself and giving yourself unkind words. We are so grateful you have taken this time to sit with us and feel our love. While you sit in the chair think about the times you didn't love yourself or you felt things were wrong and then realise you are loved and you are worthy of love. Sit in this bubble of love and kindness. Repeat the words in your mind 'I am loved'. Now stay there sitting quietly for a moment to let those words permeate though your body. 'I am loved'.

When you are ready get up and out of your temple chair knowing you can come back whenever you want to. This is your haven, your safe and special place. Open the door and close it. Walk gently back, take your time. Gradually become aware of your body. Take your time. Begin to hear the sounds around you. Wriggle your toes. Begin to move your limbs. Cover your eyes with your hands and as you gradually open them you are the first person you see. Sit quietly for a few moments feeling the love you have brought with you and keep that love and light near you as you go about your daily tasks.

June has recorded a similar channelled meditation on Love which you can access here: https://youtu.be/Blk3mxC2S6Q

What is protection?

At the beginning of every group session June makes sure people are 'grounded'. This is to protect them and to relax them, but first it's important that June asks for protection from negative energies. June asked the Angels to explain the process of protection.

'We have trouble with June. Her mind is always so busy and always concerned for others. Before a session we blow gold around her to protect her. She has been ill recently and that is because she wasn't listening. She must be protected and cover all her senses to keep her safe as she works. The ideal way to work is for her to meditate beforehand and ask us to protect her and then she must ground the group members.

June you must go up into the heavens before a session to ask us for help. Ask for two layers of gold around your aura. Imagine a light around the outside of the aura. Imagine it's gold. Keep a gold light around the outside of your body to keep you safe. People coming to you can have things like negativity around them and you don't want it to directly affect you. Negativity creates dis-ease and can affect the chakras. The grounding protection is very, very helpful'.

What is Grounding?

'In the group the grounding process is channelled through June. June asks the group members to imagine roots going from the soles of their feet to the centre of the earth. The roots travel down

through all the layers of the earth to the centre. Once the group members arrive at the centre they are asked to imagine a crystal and this will be their energy for the session. Crystals are made from the stars and we are made from the stars. The crystal energy feeds the light which will provide the energy for individual members to work with as they meditate. Even if they can't see a crystal or a light they will be affected by it. Not everyone comes to be healed they may just come to feel part of the group. Everyone is on a different stage of their journey but everyone gets the energy whether they feel it or not. They will relax and that allows us to come closer. They can then go higher into the Spiritual realms to get answers. Sometimes people have visions and sometimes people hear voices and sometimes they feel nothing except relaxation. All these effects are valuable.

At the end of the session it's important to close the session. The closing is channelled through June and we choose how this will be for the benefit of individual members. Sometimes we ask their Guardian Angels to place their hands over the individual members or we put our wings around them to protect them. That is how you might feel it but really it's about trusting us. Trust that we are there to help and we will make sure you are protected in a way suitable for you.

Most people are spiritually open whether they know it or not. Every day ask us to protect you. Take some time to meditate to feel safe in the world. Even June forgets sometimes and we find a way to remind her!

June Barclay

We always throw a golden robe over the healing room. June doesn't ask for this but we do this for her. She knows we are there to protect her'.

PART THREE

In this section of the book, we will explore different ways that our energy is embodied and how the energy of Spirit is shared with us.

June Barclay

HEALING

The following description was delivered from the Angels working with June.

'Healing is sent from the Angels in the Spirit world. If there is illness that can't be cured it's a lesson for the soul in this life.

If you feel good it helps you to enjoy life. That's the essence of wellness. Where there is darkness there is illness. Healing brings the darkness to the light. Negative emotions can block the pathways to being and feeling well.

Imagine emotion in your mind, think about being sad or happy, ill or depressed. See how it makes you feel. So healing works on the level of blocked emotions and dis-ease i.e not being at ease. You do have to love yourself and your life in order to feel well and that is sometimes very hard to do.

When healing happens we use a channel/person/healer to place their hands over your body and try to change the negative energies so you can begin to feel life is worth living again. Changes in mood and feelings of security can come from healing. it helps individuals to feel life is worth living. After a healing session people *say they feel lighter and happier even if you are living with something incurable.*

Healer/channellers are trained in a variety of ways and often work in different ways depending on that training. For example, some work directly on the body and the emotions whilst others might use crystals or cards only. Healing isn't only about making better, sometimes a healer will help someone pass over more comfortably. The healer/channeller always goes to a session with an open mind and is certain that the Spirits will be there as guides.

So you see, my dear friend, this is about faith and trust. Faith we are there to support you and trust we will love you unconditionally even if you don't love yourself.

Our reason for being is to serve and try to ease your path as God's messengers. We may have lived on earth and so we do understand how difficult it is. We may not have lived on earth but we want you to understand we are here for you always.

The healing from the Angels is from God. May our words help with your healing. We close with this remark. Our joy comes from giving you help, to make your steps lighter and we tell you that we love you and we bless you.

Q: How many sessions do I need?

J: How long is a piece of string! You leave the session and if you feel you need to return you will. It's a good idea to meditate on your experience of the session and to see if you have a feeling or a knowing that you need more. I may not be the right healer for you and if not, you will be guided to another.

Q: How long is a session?

J: Usually the first session is two hours because it's good to chat for a bit. I don't need to know what ails you, just a little about your life. After that, one hour sessions are fine.

Q: What happens in a session?

J: First of all we have a chat. I don't ask what is wrong. Sometimes your Spirit guide will tell me a bit about you. Then you lie on my couch and I keep you warm with covers and try to help you relax with some gentle music.

I sometimes rest my hands on your body and channel the Spirit world. Sometimes you will feel a tingling. You might feel more hands than mine on you. I have lots of helpers. Most times people sleep and the healing works because I get out of the way and let the healing Angels come in and let the healing happen.

It's hard for clients at the beginning to hand over their illness or dis-ease. When I am told it's time to end the session we often have another chat and a cup of tea so you are well grounded (back to normal) before you leave.

Q: How do people feel afterwards?

J: It depends on the level of healing, sometimes tired, sometimes restful, calmer or peaceful. Healing, like mediation is really about finding time for stillness in a busy world.

Her clients' experience of June's healing are profound, even when receiving it long distance over the phone from June. Sarah explained that "Not only did I feel energetic influences, I have also experienced images of healing powers. The moment was completely transformative." Whilst Julie shared that "It's hard to explain something so strong and deeply felt and when you're in the middle of the session you are almost not there at all. I felt physical sensations, some really strong and sudden, but I felt calm and safe and like there was a team of people supporting me".

The healing doesn't only help with emotional issues as Sarah continues to explain "The back pain I was suffering from has disappeared, I had the best sleep for a long time". Julie described how "After both healings I slept like a brick. The next day after both I still felt deeply relaxed and lighter at the same time. My symptoms had changed too. " Showing how both physical ailments are also affected, with phrases like "life changing" and "an amazing experience" and finally how June "has improved and enriched my life beyond my imagination".

Healing Guides

In preparing the book, June has recently discovered exactly who her healing guides are. She previously trusted that Spirit would bring the energy through her and didn't feel the need to know their identities.

The different guides are for different illnesses as each illness has a different vibration, a different source. She was told *"You don't need to know who your guide is in order for them to do their work through you."*

The build-up of light over the years that June has been working, has raised her vibration and lightened her energy allowing more guides to come in. June was told many times that she was a healer not a medium.

Whilst channeling for a Podcast June was told that "Mary" is always with her, as a Guide. "Mary" represents the three Marys from the Magdalene era, Anna (Mother of Mary, Jesus's mother) Mother Mary and Mary Magdalene. June is guided on a daily basis by this Mary Collective for the highest of her healing work .

This image of Mary was drawn by an artist friend who saw her during a session she enjoyed with June.

Mary also works with Dr B (June's not been given his full name) who works with June as a Psychic Surgeon, which means he helps remove physical ailments of her clients energetically.

Dr John, another spiritual physician, was a military surgeon in the 1800's in the Mile End Hospital. June sees him as tall and thin, wearing a Top Hat. He works independently of her during the healings but June's energy has to be in the room as she is a conduit.

June also has some other powerful Spirit helpers but has been asked by them not to identify these, suffice to say they represent all the natural healing disciplines.

In order to come into our space the spirits that work with June and other lightworkers need to assimilate their lighter energies through our denser ones in order to work and affect our world. They need us and we need to them. They need us to be as light as possible in order to enable them to work through us as it's difficult for them to come through our dense energy.

We all have guides, but those people that are lightworkers have more guides as our frequency is lighter. For the everyday Joe when things get tough and you haven't connected to anything spiritual and you ask for help, that's when the guides step in and try to guide you to a better place.

People that are not challenged by life, tend to be new souls and don't need guides. The more times you've "lived", the more Soul Growth you've done, is when you acquire the guides. Soul Growth is the reason we are here. To work with love in your heart to support those around you, is all part of Soul Growth.

Guides can be a mix of Spirit, Ancestoral Energy, Angels, Ascended Masters and Source energy. The more work you do on yourself - when you step up to the plate - your vibration raises and attracts guides. Life can get in the way, with busy lives, stress, family and work can distract you from what you need to do.

The people around you can also be your guides, earthly guides.

Who are Lightworkers?

We felt it important to expand on the term Lightworker..June believes that Lightworkers are not just people who have a direct connection to spirit like a medium or a healer, that we are ALL able to work with the light when we use our heart centre, our energy, our aura in a positive loving way to help the world. June believes that caring enough to sit in meditation and getting a connection with Spirit is working with the Light.

June emphasises that everything is from the heart, that trusting when you sit and connect to Spirit, is being a Lightworker, where you are feeling the lightness and love which will have a positive energetic impact on the world. She believes that would include Nurses & Doctors who are caring for people, or hairdressers who listen and support their customers. June says "Nothing is bigger or smaller than anyone else, it's just caring for each other."

June channels *"There are more people picking up the challenge to be Lightworkers. We can swamp the negativity with the Lightworkers, with the rate of sending out the light and also for the Lightworkers to live in the light and not have any negativity with them. You actually have to live it, to be it. At the moment there is a power struggle going on and there will always be light and dark in every situation."*

During a channeling session with Archangel Gabriel June ascertained that the meditation work we do as a group (see Appendix) is very important. When we are focusing on using healing heart energy during meditation the Angels feel this as a vibrational energy and are able to take it and use it elsewhere to help others; whether we are sitting together in a room or working together online in our homes.

As a result of this communication June confirmed that the more we raise our vibration of the heart and work in Trust, opening ourselves up to Spirit, it appears the more we help the Angels to work, spreading our positive energy where it is needed. So not only are we able to accept help from Spirit, but it now became clear that the relationship appears to be a two way one..

CRYSTALS

Crystals are formed from minerals and they occur naturally in the Earth's surface. The healing, life-enhancing powers of crystals have been recorded in many ancient texts, from the Bible to traditional Chinese medicine and Ayurvedic books. They have an innate energy that can benefit you, those around you, your home and your workspace. They may improve your general state of wellbeing, dispel negative energy and speed up positive changes in your life.

Crystals can help you to focus and clear the mind for meditation. Regular meditation with crystals will help your mind unwind, and also bring more energy and creativity to your thoughts

Birthstone Crystals

It is said that carrying your birthstone connects you with the vibration of the universe as it was when you were born. This brings protection, good fortune, health and longevity.

CAPRICORN *(Dec 22nd – Jan 19th)* - **GARNET**
Known as the 'daydreamer', Garnet is believed to regenerate body systems – especially the bloodstream where it is also a good purifier. It is also strongly associated with the balancing of sex drive and emotional disharmony. It is believed to be aligned to the base chakra. It can bring love, compassion and an enhanced imagination.

AQUARIUS *(Jan 20th – Feb 18th)* – **AMETHYST**
Admired for its beauty, this semi-precious stone is known for its spirituality and used extensively for healing and meditation. It is said by mystics that sleeping with Amethyst can promote intuitive dreams and astral travel. This powerful crystal facilitates transmutation of lower energies into the higher frequencies of both the spiritual and ethereal levels.

PISCES *(Feb 19th – Mar 20th)* – **AQUAMARINE**
This crystal teaches us to be fearless in all things and to embrace age. To value the wisdom that comes with it and to create your own luck and happiness. Aquamarine provides us with the courage to be calm, whatever the circumstance, and consider our actions.

ARIES *(Mar 21st – Apr 19th)* – **RED JASPER**
Red Jasper makes a good worry bead and a few tumbled in the pocket have a surprisingly remarkable effect on our emotions. It provides insight into the most difficult of problems. It helps stabilise the energy field around the body and has a cleansing

effect on the aura. The energy of Jasper is beneficial to the kidneys, spleen, bladder, liver, stomach and womb.

TAURUS *(Apr 20th – May 20th)* – **ROSE QUARTZ**
Known as the 'inner peace' stone, Rose Quartz is widely believed to emit a calming, cooling energy that works on all the chakras to gently remove negativity and reinstate the calm, gentle force of self-love. It restores tranquility and clarity after times of chaos or crisis.

GEMINI *(May 21st – Jun 21st)* – **CITRINE**
Citrine is a crystal that does not hold negative energy. It is able to take negativity and ground it. Hence it never needs to be cleansed. This crystal works on the solar plexus chakra. It communicates on the etheric as an early warning system, alerting us that self-protection is necessary and allowing us to place barriers before an attack.

CANCER *(Jun 22nd – Jul 22nd)*– **MOONSTONE**
Feminine and calming, emotional and loving, this smooth, milky mineral is said to be a reflection of the Moon goddess herself, encapsulated on Earth for the good of humankind. It is used for many 'women's problems', period pains, tensions, pregnancy and breastfeeding mothers.

LEO *(Jul 23rd – Aug 22nd)* – **CARNELIAN**
Carnelian provides perception and awakens our talents by channelled inspiration. It is an excellent stone for daydreamers

because it sharpens the concentration and helps reduce absentmindedness. It dispels apathy and mental lethargy. As a healing tool, Carnelian works on all the chakras below the heart and is useful in the treatment of rheumatism, arthritis and neuralgia.

VIRGO *(Aug 23rd – Sep 22nd)* – **PERIDOT**
Known as the 'release' stone, Peridot helps us to allow ourselves to let go of unnecessary burdens or baggage. It is believed to be an excellent antitoxin gemstone. It cleans most organs and glands and is a good overall tonic for the body and mind. It reduces stress, accelerates personal growth, stimulates the mind and opens new levels of awareness and opportunity.

LIBRA *(Sep 23rd – Oct 23rd)*– **KYANITE**
The Blue Kyanite is used for healing and strengthening the throat and larynx. It is well known as a friend to singers and performers. It aligns all chakras naturally and is particularly successful with the crown, third eye and throat chakras. The blades of Kyanite allow us to cut through illusion by working within the dimensions that structure one's thinking.

SCORPIO *(Oct 24th – Nov 21st)* – **MALACHITE**
Malachite protects us from radiation and enhances the immune system and is often used in jewellery exactly for this reason. Malachite also raises our sensitivity and awareness of 'spirit guides', helping us to cultivate our psychic abilities. It can remove

past traumas, and negative emotional hurt, bringing harmony into your life.

SAGITTARIUS *(Nov 22nd – Dec 21st)* – **SODALITE**
Sodalite eliminates confusion, enabling us to find our 'truth' in all situations and weight it against the truth of others. It acts on the brow and throat chakras with a slow, pulsing energy that calms and clarifies. It also helps us to recognise and deal with rigid thought patterns that lurk within our nature. Sodalite helps with phobias and calms panic attacks.

How do you use Crystals?

Crystals are often used in meditation and healing but there is a great deal of confusion about what is a useful crystal and what might not be. June asked the Angels to explain a little about their use. Uriel came through:

'Crystals are just a tool to lighten the atmosphere and to bring the light. They are immensely powerful and used in the wrong hands can be quite dangerous. People use crystals for healing and for scrying (e.g. looking into a crystal ball to see the future). They can be used as a support and to help with a problem but too many at one time can be unhelpful. It's important to get the right balance. It's easy to read the books and use too many at one time. The best way is to be guided to use them. Ask your Guardian Angel whether a particular crystal is the right one for you. You can do this through meditation or by using a dowser and asking. Try running your hands over the crystals and see if one has a stronger

energy than another. Your Guardian Angel is always with you and knows what is best for you. So if you feel you are reaching for a crystal that you are unfamiliar with then you are probably being guided to use it.

Crystals are like you, they need to be looked after. They need sunshine and they need to be cleansed and they definitely need to be loved. As they support you, it is your part to support them. They take the negativity from you and they bring the light when you channel the Angel realms.

If you put one near a computer or television or anything electronic the crystal needs a great deal more care. Clean them regularly. Please do not have them in your bedroom unless you are sure that crystal is the right one for you as they can cause insomnia if they do not suit you.

You can make an elixir from the crystals by soaking them in water and then drinking the water that may be a better way for you to take in the energy.

Before a healing session the healer asks whether the crystals to be used are the right ones for the person to be healed and where they should be placed. It can distort the healing if the crystals are wrong. If the crystal is not well cleaned it can pass on the negativity to the person to be healed. There is a great deal to be done to care for crystals. Wash them regularly in clean slightly soapy water and leave them in the sun to dry. Be mindful and think about how you want to use them.

I leave you with my love and support. God bless and keep you safe'.

The following is a picture of a Healing Table laid with crystals especially for the book. They are there to help with healing and to be sure the book resonates with you. Each crystal holds a blessing from the Angels involved in writing this book:

CHAKRAS

The chakras are vortices of subtle energy within the human aura like spinning wheels – an electromagnetic field of varying vibrational frequencies. There are seven principal chakras which each correlate to a different part of the body– the Base Chakra, the Sacral Chakra, the Solar Plexus Chakra, the Heart Chakra, the Throat Chakra, the Brow Chakra and the Crown Chakra.

Through these chakras flows incoming information that is of great benefit to our health, especially in stimulating and fine-tuning the actions of the endocrine glands and major body organs. These glands produce hormones, which in turn affect the whole body, ideally bringing about a balanced state of health and mind.

Each Chakra has a colour, which follow the colours of the rainbow. The colours change in intensity as our emotions change.

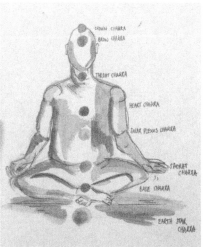

Chakra meanings

CROWN (violet)
The Crown Chakra is the source of our spirituality and our connection to the universe, imagination and awareness It is responsible for the transcendence of our limitations allowing access to the utmost clarity, enlightened wisdom & Higher Self.

BROW/THIRD Eye (indigo)
The Brow Chakra is about opening our mind and being open to ideas, thoughts and dreams. Our extra sensory perception, intuition and physic abilities all originate from here.

THROAT (blue)
The Throat Chakra is about communication, the ability to speak with love, kindness and truth. Also being able to express ourselves openly and authentically.

HEART (green)
The Heart Chakra is where our love (for self and others), compassion and kindness originate. It also enables us to forgive others and ourselves. It's green colour is all about healing and health.

SOLAR PLEXUS (yellow)
The Solar Plexus Chakra is where we hold our personal power, it's the physical centre of our emotions and where our personal power is born. It holds our sense of identity and self-confidence.

SACRAL (orange)
The Sacral Chakra is about our identity as a human and our connection to other people. It's the home of creativity and life force energy, which helps us to enjoy our time on Earth. It holds an energy that motivates us to enjoy the fruits of our labour.

BASE (red)
The base chakra is all about our connection to the Earth, grounding our energy so that we feel stable and secure. It's about survival, strength, ambition and abundance with the ability to move forward in life.

Healing with crystals

You place the crystals on the chakras focusing energy directly where needed for healing. Crystals can also be placed on specific areas to help ease pain or discomfort. When all chakras are balanced many benefits can be felt. A healthy chakra is in balance and full of moving energy. Where there is dis-ease, the energy slows or becomes blocked. Working with chakras can heal and prevent dis-ease, promoting physical, mental and Spiritual health.

Lie down and place the following crystals on the chakras, lie still for 30 minutes rest and relax. Ideally repeat this exercise daily.

Crown Chakra *(top of the head)*
AMETHYST – A natural tranquiliser, relieving stress & strain. Balances mood swings, dispels fear and anxiety whilst dissolving negativity.

Brow Chakra *(centre of forehead above the eyebrow)*
LAPIS LAZULI – A deep calming energy and a strong connection to cosmic wisdom, helping you alight with universal quality of truth and integrity.

Throat Chakra *(centre of throat)*
BLUE LACE AGATE – A great nurturing and supportive stone. Also a powerful throat healer, assisting you with verbal expression of thoughts and feelings.

Heart Chakra *(centre of the chest)*
ADVENTURINE – A calming and healing crystal that helps to protect the heart, harmonising any negative emotions that often gets stuck, it also encourages compassionate behaviour.

Solar Plexus Chakra *(behind the soft cartilage at bottom of the breastbone)*
CITRINE – A positive, optimistic stone, it helps to promote motivation, and activate creativity, encouraging self-expression and helping to cultivate confidence & personal power.

Sacral Chakra *(just below the navel)*
CARNELIAN – A stabilizing stone which helps to restore vitality

and motivation, whilst stimulating creativity. It promotes positive life choices and dispels apathy.

<u>Base Chakra</u> *(the coccyx at the base of the spine)*
RED JASPER – A calming and balancing crystal that increases emotional stability& protection whilst offering self-confidence, courage and balance.

ENERGY

What is an Aura?

The general definition of one's Aura, is an emotional, mental and spiritual energy field that surrounds the body. Auras can hold different colours at different times and become bigger or smaller depending on the emotional & spiritual state of the person.

When discussed with June, she explains that in our highest energy form through healing, working with spirit or love, she sees Auras shine bright but with distress and trauma it dulls and becomes close to their body, becoming more compact. She explains that by meditating, working from the heart or working with intuition, helps to expand your aura energy, what June calls "sitting in your own power" and how we are able to change how we feel as a result.

Here you can see, using a process known as Kirlian Photography, how the energy of the Aura can appear:

During discussion with June we looked at how our gut or intuition relates to the Solar Plexus Chakra and if this in turn is connected with our Aura colour or vibration. June channeled;

"You feel the emotion first in the Solar Plexus which raises to the Heart to open the Heart, which then goes to the throat. The Chakras if they are in line and in connection, this is where you would feel this feeling. The Aura goes out to meet, sensing, but the real knowing is in the Chakra"

June translated this by saying we already have the knowing in the Chakra, because the Aura has gone out first and sensed who you would talk to first in the room for example, this sensation then goes from the gut, to the heart and on to the throat. So the Aura is the antenna with the vibration going to the Chakra, then the gut kicks in.

What are Orbs?

From her experience of talking with other Spirit workers, June thinks that she is one of the few Mediums who can see Orbs, circles of light that indicate a spirit was present.

June first saw Stuart as an Orb when she lived in Hope Cove. This circle of light would follow her down the corridor and when she reached her office she would receive a call from her other son Carl to say he was on his way home or something else important would happen.

A family friend, Jill who lost their son John in a car crash after he returned from a tour in Afghanistan. Family photos after that would often have light orbs on them, which they believe was their son's spirit making his presence known (see photos)

June feels the orb is about how the spirit travel. She channels *"That's our vehicle, the Orb. Our vehicle for showing ourselves to you, it's a condensed energy. As you know we're everywhere, we can be in lots of places at one time. But maybe you don't always see that energy and an Orb condenses it"*

June explained how often, when channeling a message for a client, she will see their Spirit messengers as Orbs, which will give a flash of light within themselves, to confirm that June has given the right message. She reads this as an affirmation through their light energy.

It is possible that this light & energy of the Orb in Spirit may translate to the Aura we have now on Earth and that when we pass over, the light of our Aura becomes our Spirit Orb.

VIBRATION

W hen looking at healing and all the modalities that can help support you physically, emotionally and spiritually, it's helpful to look at them as vibrational frequencies. It is through these frequencies that the angels are able to help us and connect with our own personal vibrations.

On a rainy day in June's Healing Hut she connected with Stuart to ask him about being a vibrational being.

"You are a denser quality than we are. You have to be dense to live on the Earth plane, it's almost what holds us here, the denseness, it's solid matter. The only part of you that is light vibration is your soul, your soul is the part which leaves your body when you go home and the soul is the light being, the light vibration."

June asked Stuart if we needed to raise our vibration in order to communicate with Spirit, he responded:

"It's more about allowing spirit into your life. You do raise it, but there is a great deal of work to do that, it's too much to explain. Do you understand that? Do you understand what that would take to raise your vibration? It's possible for people like my Mum as this is her job. Her contract with me, is for her to raise her vibration, to join me. Not me to join her"

June told Stuart that we had been exploring the concept of vibration for the book, about the many forms of vibration such as crystals, sound and colour being some of them. He replied:

"Even the book is vibration, do you understand that?. The paper and words are solid but it came from a place of vibration, for those words to be put on paper. The book has a vibration all of its own as it's been written by Spirit."

Colour

Every colour that we can see, in the seven spectrum, has a special power, quality and essence all its own, and when used in healing can balance and amplify the energetic body, comprised of the chakras and the subtle body or aura.

We can be influenced by colour in so many ways in our everyday lives. The vibrations of colour can nourish our cells and organs, from the food we eat, the clothes we wear to the colours of our environment; this can be the walls of our home or the colours of nature.

Each colour has a separate vibration that is able to help us and enhance our sense of wellbeing. The blue of the sky and the green of the trees or the red of the rose and the yellow of the daffodil, can have a profound impact on our sense of balance and wellbeing.

We took the opportunity one day when June was channeling Archangel Raziel to ask him about the vibration of colour, he shared that:

"The colour and vibration go together. You are vibrational being, and the colour that you choose to wear, will either raise your spirits or dampen your spirits. Going back to nature there are wonderful colours; there is every shade of green, of pink, of violet, every shade of red and orange. And I'm telling you because there are the 7 colours of rainbow, the 7 colours of chakras.

The vibration you put into your body or onto your body is important. I walk with the colours of the rainbow and I work with the colours of the rainbow and there are mysteries in your world you will never understand, but until you point these facts out to the human race, they will be blind or deaf to what there is on offer and by that I mean closed down to everything that is beautiful. The wonders of your world are important to every soul that lives on the earth plane, they just have to open their eyes to see them and maybe they need to be guided and shown the facts."

Using the principle of Chromotherapy shows that the colours we surround ourselves with resonate with the colours of our chakras, which represent both our connection to our own inner wisdom and to spirit on different levels whilst also embodying our own physical state of health.

In June's work she is drawn to wear a variety of colours and is often aware of how this impacts her work. If she is drawn to wear blue for a client she knows that it's about communication (throat chakra) or if she picks pink flowers for the room she knows it's about working with the heart chakra. This symbiotic relationship helps the healing frequencies of healers and Spirit to raise the vibration of the person they are working with where needed.

During an interview June channelled from Stuart that each chakra colour also becomes part of one's Aura, creating a rainbow effect around them. Although one colour tends to dominate this multi-coloured vibrational border, the remaining colours still exist within it. An Aura colour will correlate with the meaning of the chakra colour, for example if you are creative then the colour would be orange (sacral) or if you are the spiritual then the colour would be violet (crown).

When June asked Stuart about how the colour of the Aura appears, he confirmed that *"in the moment, the most dominant colour will be seen. The dominant colour, eg: spirituality is violet, but this does not mean you are out of balance as the other colours are still there. Every colour holds all the colours within it".*

If you find yourself drawn to a particular colour or resisting certain colours, it may be worth looking at which chakra this colour represents and see if the abundance, or absence of these qualities, resonates in your life at that time.

During this channelled session Stuart also confirmed that Spirit see us as colour, as we vibrate as colours. June was shown that when someone needs healing, Spirit put the colour back into the body and that they *"class the blue as the healing colour and we also know that it's also connected to the throat".*

Apparently during a healing they look at all the colours round the body and notice if any of them are depleted or broken it shows a point of illness, as they don't see us as a person. Stuart also added that *"do we realise that the organs need a different colour, so that is the connection to the chakra. The colour of the chakra, connects to the organs that are near it."*

Sound

During the channeling session with Archangel Raziel June also asked him about the vibration of sound and how it can help us. He explained:

"Listening to the right music makes a Human being, if it's the right music, makes them feel calm or puts them into a happy place and can almost make them grounded by dancing on the earth. So I would say that sound is very important. People as long as they've lived on the Earth plane have made music of some description and this music changes their vibration. If they're sad they play sad music to make them cry. If they're happy, the music makes their heart open and gives them a sense of wellbeing and brings them joy.

So sound is very important. Hearing someone sing the words or somebody with comforting words when you're not well. [bird starts to sing outside] *and you listen to the birds song and how does that make you feel? You are grateful for our winged beings, they are beauty in nature, their colours, the way they fly. I would say that sound is important."*

NATURE

When considering the topic of vibration and frequency it is a natural conclusion that all of Nature has its own vibration from the grass and clouds to plants and water. June asked Stuart about the impact that Nature has on us:

"Nature is your food, air, water. Nature is the breath of life. Nature is Nurture. Human race has lost its way. People who live in tower blocks don't realise the importance of being out in nature. There's nothing more profound than standing on beach, sand in your toes, walking through the sea. Humankind has turned to monetary gain and think that that's their growth, but actually stepping back and away from all things monetary and being in nature is your God given right. [started to rain heavily] *Rain is nature. Do you want the flowers to grow?!"*

Vibrational Medicine

June ask Stuart if he could talk about the link between the vibration of Nature and vibrational medicine. She explains to the interviewer that he is showing her a pathway with a tall yellow flower and how this flower then becomes a remedy, leading onto being an Essence, then Aromatherapy Oils and leading on again to Homeopathy.

This pathway supports the principle of using plants and components of the Earth in healing and working with the vibration of the natural element. This vibration is demonstrated by Scientists, who have not only used Kirlian photography to demonstrate the human aura, but as you can see in this diagram, plants have them as well:

J- So is nature more about wellbeing than reaching Spirit?

"Nature is about wellbeing but being in nature is where spirit can access you easily. The smell of a flower and I may say a rose, opens the heart. Have you never connected the feeling of smelling a flower to how your heart feels? And why do you think men give women red roses?"

June explained that she understood that when we open our heart, that's how Spirit access us, it's their "in" to us.

Roses

The theme of the rose has run through this book thanks to Stuart and June feels that the rose is the "heart opener" in Nature, it is one of the ways that Spirit is able to communicate with us, through the vibration of the flower,

A dear friend of June's, Katy Gostick, uses her connection with roses to embody this vibrational relationship we all have with nature. Having always loved roses since her childhood, where her parent's garden was filled with much admired varieties, she came to have a more esoteric understanding of the healing energy of this powerful flower through meeting a rose Alchemist, Sandy Humby.

She explains that "The energy of the rose is a healing gift from the Divine and their words are to help us connect with the different stories held within each of us and to help remove, dissolve or change those stories, if they are not serving our highest potential.

To give a little more context to this source of healing; the rose originally came from Persia, although there has been evidence of fossilised roses as far back as 32 million years ago.

The fragrance of the rose has been captured and preserved in the form of rose water by an ancient method that can be traced back to biblical times in the Middle East, and later to the Indian subcontinent. There are also strong links with Mary Magdalene and the "Way of the Rose" which embodies both the Divine Feminine and the Divine Masculine as they flow together. According to Ishtara Rose, High Priestess of the Magdalene "The Way of the Rose is ultimately the path of self-worth, for if within us all we were balanced with profound self-love the world would be a very different place."

The rose has often been described as a "Gift from God" and has been known for centuries to symbolise Love. It also embodies the Fibonnaci series, which is derived from the Golden Ratio; which is nature's efficiency scale and is the foundation of all life, proof of order and regularity in the universe, illustrating further its sacred significance.

Katy uses the vibrational energy of the rose to channel messages from various Angels and Ascended Masters and in order to "assist in opening your heart centre to the love that is available to you and to help you to release all that no longer serves you and all that holds you back from being the truly amazing being that you are."

Katy kindly shared one of the messages she channelled in her 21 Sacred Rose Blessings, that she felt was pertinent to the recurring messages in this book. She suggests that if you wish, you could hold your left hand over the image of the rose and place your right hand over your heart, then slowly read the words. Breathe gently and imagine and allow the essence, energy and image of the rose to find its way into your heart centre.

THE ROSE OF WISDOM
"Love is all there is"

I am the Rose of Wisdom and my colour will enhance your light when you place me in your heart. I will help connect you with your own inner wisdom and the golden light of God/Divine Source energy which is in all of you.

Each and every one of you has an innate inner wisdom that is at the centre of your being, this wisdom is in essence the collective golden energy that surrounds you at all times, it is the Universal energy field that is supporting humankind on the Earth plane at this time. We would encourage each and every one of you to accept this as a Truth and to accept and feel into your own knowing and inner wisdom.

When you can trust your own wisdom, when you walk with love and integrity every day, when you trust that you are One with the Universe and supported at all times, you become a being of light. As such you will begin to flow with God/Source Energy or you may call it Universal Wisdom but it matters not what words you use as you will be working with the energy and essence of love.

CONNECTING WITH SPIRIT

What are Angel Cards and oracle cards and how do I use them?

Angel cards are a wonderful way to invite Angels into your life. Keep them on display in a bowl and choose one at random for a daily affirmation.

Firstly, choose a set of oracle cards that resonate with you, centre yourself, sit quietly and take a few deep breaths. Imagine a brilliant ray of light beaming through from the earth to the heavens. This allows you to be grounded and then protect yourself from negative or distracting energies from other people. Imagine that you are in a protective bubble and it is a force field, repelling any negative energy.

Fill your cards with love, take the deck in your hands, and hold it to your heart and bless them. Shine a light into what you would like to ask the Angels help with, what area of your life and a specific question. Shuffle the cards, to imprint your energy on them. If you are reading for a friend, ask them to shuffle the cards.

Then fan out the cards on a table and choose a card using your non-dominant hand, your fingers may tingle or feel warm over the card(s) that you are meant to pick. Also pay attention to any that 'jump' out during the shuffle, and whenever several are stuck together.

When you turn a card over, think what it means to you, be aware of your first feeling, image, or insight that comes up for you. Trust your intuition, because your first impulse is usually the best. Additionally, you may wish to look at the list of meanings in the booklet that normally accompanies the oracle cards if you require any further insight, but always trust your first thoughts.

Using a pendulum for contacting Spirit

Anyone can use a pendulum it just takes a bit of practice. You don't need to spend a lot of money you can start by choosing a weight on a chain. You might use an existing necklace you like or find something you like to attach to a chain or even a key. The important thing is the weight hangs symmetrically and is not magnetic.

How does the pendulum work?

Many people watching someone using a pendulum are suspicious the user is moving the pendulum. It's important for the user to practice as much as possible to avoid this happening. Some people say its actions reflect an intuition, others are sure it is contact with Spirit. It provides answers to questions and the most useful way to use it is to ask Spirit questions that can be answered with a yes or no. If Spirit doesn't know the answer or is not sure it either won't move at all or move in circles

How do I use the pendulum?

First energetically clean the pendulum by leaving it in the sun for a day and then hold it in your hand.

Start by sitting somewhere quietly and stilling your mind by deep breathing and then concentrating on the flow of breath in and out of your nose. Wait until you are feeling relaxed. Ask Spirit if it will use the pendulum and ask them to bless it. Hold the chain of the pendulum firmly across your fingers so it hangs still. Ask Spirit if it will show you a yes sign and then a no sign. These may be different for each pendulum and so it's important to ask. The pendulum will either moved backwards and forwards and side to side. Some pendulums move in circles for yes or no so it's advisable to practice calmly and slowly at first. Both Spirit and you need to get used to this new form of communication so be patient it takes time and at first the movement may be imperceptible.

What questions can I ask?

Once you have established the direction of answer you can ask Spirit some questions. Ask simple questions to practice. 'Is my name Jane?' 'Do I have a car?'.

Keep practicing, just relax and have some fun. Ask it to help you find something. You can ask 'is it in the bedroom?' or 'is it in the kitchen?'.

As time goes on you can ask more emotion-based questions. 'Am I eating the right foods for my body?' 'Should I trust Mary?'.

It's not working what should I do?

First of all relax, this is normal. It may be that you are feeling upset today. You could be sitting near electrical items that are creating an alternative energy field. Try phrasing a question differently. Put the pendulum away and start again tomorrow.

Keep your pendulum in a silk purse or special container.

Signs from the Angels

June has always had the sensation of an itchy nose, which eventually she realised were the Angels giving her a sign that they were near and as a precursor to a message. Because June isn't always paying attention the Angels feel the need to use this sensation to get June to focus on them. Of late she has had her hair pulled as well, but this is only when Jesus is in the room. June also feels incredibly hot when she is channelling.

Spirit is always there for us and often provides comfort through signs that we can see and relate to.

Feathers

Feathers are a popular way for Angels to make themselves known. Lisa says that she often sees *"White feathers floating*

89

down in front of me or nearby give a comforting reassurance that spirit love ones are close to me, giving me encouragement to keep going when things are tough." Whilst Katie has *"always been aware of white feathers in my path. It's funny how they appear when I'm thinking about something and take them as a sign that I'm on the right path."*

As a universal symbol for Angels on your path it soon becomes a way of life for people, as Bianca *explains "As a family we look for signs from the spirit world. I am always aware of feathers in my path indicating presence of angels."* And they can often turn up in unexpected places as Joanna explains *"For me whenever i see a feather on its own, where you wouldn't expect it, I always feel it's a sign from the Angels to connect with me. I always pick up the feather and put it in my pocket as a token of love from the Angels."*

<u>Birds & Butterflies</u>

For other people they find that animals are the signs that Angels choose. June often gets butterflies before she gets a message or a call, as they fly close and follow her around.

Birds can often remind people of loved ones who've passed over as Katie *says "I also take birds as signs that Spirit is with me, especially the cheeky robin, who I mainly think is my Mum who died 25 years ago."* Bianca has a *"strong bond with robins and butterflies. I feel my dad is the robin and close by when I am in the garden."* And Joanna explained that *"Whenever I see a robin it reminds me of my Grandad in spirit which gives me great comfort and a big smile on my face as though he is looking down at me from heaven, and always say hello to him."*

They can also offer reassurance that you are on the right path, Lisa says that *"Two robins that visit my garden regularly, give a sense of calm to me, everything will be ok, whilst butterflies make me feel very blessed and thankful."* or confirm you have made the right decision as Bianca explains *"I feel my husband's wife Wendy (and mother to our son) who passed away 12 years ago often visits us in the form of a butterfly. When I adopted Charlie 5 years ago, the confirmation letter from the courts came through the door and John and I were both sitting at the dining room table. It was November and all the windows were shut. As soon as we opened the letter a red admiral butterfly appeared and landed on the dining room table. We were both in tears and I saw it as a confirmation from Wendy that she was happy about it."*

Sometimes it's the way in which loved ones remind you that they are always nearby, Julie says *"I see butterflies on many occasions that remind me or connect me with my lovely mum that passed away nearly 4 years ago. From a white one appearing whilst we are on a private boat far out to sea in Italy, to a random butterfly hair clip in my coat pocket I never knew was there whilst on a lonely walk. I was also driven to emptying a whole drawer of stationery to unearth a card hand made by my mother for me I had never seen...had a happy message to me and...a butterfly on the front!"*

Sounds & Sensations

For some people they are able to feel more subtle signs, like Lisa who says she *"Often I get the feeling of someone stroking my hair, it's not scary in any way. It makes me feel that I'm not alone and is very comforting."* Or Joanna who shares that she can sometimes *"feel a tingling sensation on the side of my face to remind me that my Guardian angel is close by, a sign to guide me to follow my feelings rather than what you think you should be doing."*

Spirit can also use sensations to show they are helping the person to work as Bianca explains *"I feel spirit rather than see or hear. It is a knowing. I feel my guardian angel on the right side of my face tingling and a tingling in my left side of upper back for a spirit guide I call Savannah. They are both very comforting. When I am doing my reflexology my shoulders feel intensely hot like someone has their hands or wings on me helping me. I think it is Stuart as it is strongest when I'm doing June's feet."* Or when they themselves are receiving healing as Julie says that she *"yawns a lot when spirit is close and healing me or other folk nearby. That's when I ask direct for help or healing."*

Spirit will also use methods that we can relate to such as sound. Natasha finds that *"Mostly my loved ones in Spirit communicate through music. A song that reminds me of them often plays when I need a reassurance or cheering up. The most prominent time was when I was driving down a lane and a song came on that reminded me of a friend who had died in a motorcycle accident. Although it was only a lane, I knew he was telling me I had to slow down so I did. Straight afterwards a deer jumped out from the hedge right in front of me, through the hedge on the other side (he went through the air, didn't even touch the road). Had I not slowed down he would have hit my windscreen.....* " and Bianca agrees that *"Music is also very important with songs coming on the radio that are just not coincidental. We all just have to look out for the signs."*

There are no avenues unexplored by Spirit, Christina says that she *"often smells things. It can be flowers, perfume and recently I had the odd sense of smelling wet dogs downstairs in the afternoon and evening. Perhaps it was because I had spoken to my daughter and their family that day and felt close to them all. I am not sure but I could definitely smell their dogs Charlie and Barnie as if they had been in the rain."*

We will visit this later and how these signs can help people deepen their spiritual practice and help them on their life's journey.

June Barclay

PART FOUR

In this section Stuart introduces the idea of opening our hearts to the Spirit world and allowing Spirit to protect and guide us through our lives. Using testimony from people who have worked with June and some who work with Stuart the reader will be guided to better understand how Spirit can help and how some people have found that help life affirming.

June Barclay

A WORD FROM STUART

Opening the heart

We asked June to ask Stuart to begin part three of this book. During the time he was talking through her they chatted to each other. Sometimes Stuart is frustrated about making sure his contribution is clear and understandable. He has information he wants to impart and he is clear when we have got it right. The experience of this for all the people in the room is that our heads feel an intense pressure, an urgency that must be reduced because it's uncomfortable. As June begins to concentrate on exactly what Stuart is saying the pressure reduces until we feel the message from him has been completed. He chose the title for this section.

June, once again, sat quietly on her sofa, hands resting gently in her lap and her eyes closed.

'There is no such word as completion when working with Spirit (Here he means the Spirit world including both people who have passed over and the Angels). *It is a never-ending journey. You grow in Spirit as you grow on the earth plane. Your journey and*

the reward you feel is to become closer to Spirit, your helper and your guide (here he means your chosen guardian Angel who is there for you from birth to death). *This Spirit will love you unconditionally beyond whatever love is to you now. As you work with Spirit you begin to realise you are waking in the morning and you will feel you love yourself first, before anybody else.*

From me to you today I'd like to say you are the most important person in your life. Of all the people walking on the earth plane you are first. If this isn't the case, how can you give from an empty space and how can you receive from an empty space. You have to do the work on yourself first.

I just want you to breathe the joy of living on the earth plane. Look at the beauty. Even in the saddest moments there is beauty. Sometimes in the deepest darkest times there will be a spark of light to guide you if you take the time to ask and listen to or watch for the answer. This listening and observing will help you to grow and feel confidence and happiness even when you feel things are going wrong.

Do not look at sadness and grief, obstructions and negativity, as the end. With these experiences you start your real journey; the real journey that makes you who you are. I'd like you to know that Spirit is in the sunshine and rain and in the wind and in every season. Spirit will be standing there and waiting. Spirit only sees beauty where you might see darkness'.

Here June said there was a crowd of Spirits and Angels in the room and she wished she could take a photograph as the colours they brought with them were wonderful. Stuart interrupted and asked her to continue.

'You know Mum it is only about love. From now on everything we do is about opening the heart. The queue you see are Spirits waiting in line to support humanity.

Here June laughed with her son. 'He says *'Let's get this show on the road!* He is dangling keys and saying these are the keys to the heart ready to be used for the benefit of anyone who asks.'

THE JOURNEY

Many of the people who have come in contact with the Spirit world started slowly. They gradually built up their awareness of other realities and spent more time with their own thoughts and with reading about other people's experiences. The value for individuals taking some time out of their busy schedules to focus on themselves seems to have the side effect of improving their sense of self-worth and their interactions with others. They found they began to feel more compassionate, became more aware of other people's life difficulties and increased their tolerance of people that they may have previously have found difficult. They discovered a new understanding of their world.

Finding a sense of peace is often a primary goal in our lives. Stuart has said that it is just a question of listening to our Guides, our Guardian Angels, our Spirits. Don't get too muddled about these words. Many people think they are interchangeable. Others say Spirits are people who have lived and died and Angels are higher beings teachers and guides. Just sit a while and you will come to know and decide for yourself who you are talking to. Initially this feels so unrealistic. Sitting in a quiet room waiting for something to happen can seem an odd way of spending time. Walking towards and working with Spirit is not easy. However, the value of recognising we are not alone, that we have Guardian Angels just waiting to surround us with unconditional love, is surely worth the initial effort to try to make contact.

Some people are aware of Spirit from the time they are born. Others fall into crisis and cry out for help. Whatever the journey to Spirit, the value of finding your way to work with them in your daily life is both comforting and life enhancing.

We interviewed men, women and young people who have taken this journey to try to understand the many different ways they had experienced Spirit in their lives. As a result of interviews, themes emerged which described both individual journeys and the extra benefits people had gained by working hard to understand themselves and listen. The themes follow a journey into Spirit:

- Introductions - that is how the interviewees began to become more familiar with Spirit;

- Finding ways to work with Spirit and how Spirit worked with them. It includes the various different approaches people used to find their connection to Spirit

- Other benefits - the other benefits that came from this work;

- The critical voice - how each person has dealt with people who find these concepts difficult or absurd; and finally,

- Opening the heart - how continued focus on Guardian Angels has led to an opening of their own hearts and an understanding of the true meaning of love.

Introductions

The interviewees described the routes they chose to become aware of the Spirit world. For some it was a general feeling of having lost a life path, a recognition that life was unsatisfactory which so often led to feeling alone. As Jennie said:

'I was very stressed and had a poor self-image. I was a mum and always put myself last but through the meditation I recognised my self-worth. Over time I began to see things, colours and impressions. I'd started to wake early in the mornings and find I had the answers to challenges I was having'.

For others a life break caused by the end of one employment and the beginning of another meant there were choices to be made. Taking some time to consider what those choices were provided Lou with a much-needed breathing space,

'I have not had this opportunity to re-group for years and it's given me valuable time to work out where I want to go next. To be not doing anything and have no need to check my phone is alien for me, but I feel much more grounded and centered as a result'.

Mary went to see June at a time when her life was very difficult and she felt she had lost her way,

> 'When I came to Devon with the girls I was exhausted and I instantly felt this huge blanket of love and it reconnected me with my Spiritual path. June gave me some healing and guidance from the Angels, it was priceless. She gave me hope and that everything was going to work out ok. It has helped me so much through last year and this year when I have had my tough days. I just keep remembering what June told me and the Footprints verse'.

Sue also had help from June. She had very bad back pain and June noticed this.

> 'Oh dear she said ... your back still isn't right! She immediately put her hands on my back, and I had a feeling that something was squashed out of me, I came over really emotional, like a big release and couldn't stop crying with this lady that I had never met before'.

Joan had been truly suffering with multiple symptoms and her life was being slowly eroded by the various tests and treatments she was trying. Various doctors had suggested diagnoses but none seemed to describe the whole picture

> 'I contacted June whilst I was experiencing serious symptoms of Lyme disease and Dengue Fever and I was struggling with what I later discovered was a burst cyst on my liver that had held further trauma',

She describes the moment she turned to June for help

'We made contact and her voice made me feel immediately at ease by firstly acknowledging my trauma of what I was going through. Most folk around me thought I was making it up, I cried a lot with relief that finally someone could help me. She then offered to clear layer by layer what was going on for me with the help of 'upstairs'.

Recently Joan contacted June to say she had been cleared of the Lyme disease that had been the physical cause for her symptoms.

Martin, who really didn't believe in a Spirit world was sceptical but also in pain and alarmed about his symptoms. On the advice of his wife he phoned June.

'She asked me to think of some nice things and she left me hanging on the phone for a couple of minutes which made me feel odd because I am a sceptic, she then came back and said she had been meditating and thinking of my situation and said yes you do have prostate cancer in the right side and it will all be fine... a few weeks later we found out the cancer was only in the right side of the gland so its 50/50 and she didn't need to say it was in the right side but she was so definite'.

Eleanor was already interested in the possibility of reincarnation, but it took a life crisis for her to take the time to think about how her life had, as she describes, gone wrong.

'I've always been fascinated by ideas such as reincarnation and the 'meaning of life' but was triggered to explore these areas further about 25 years after the breakdown of my first marriage (at my instigation) after only a year. I was very low and in a lot of doubt about my own judgement and confused as to how I made such a mistake in marrying the wrong person'.

Many people are aware of Spirits. Often very young children will talk about beings they have seen walking alongside them only to have their experiences dismissed by adults. Knowing there is more to life than that which we see in front of our eyes helped Lisa and Leila to recognise the value of studying further what they already knew.

'I feel I have always been Spiritually connected from a young child, communicating with nature, insects and animals. I was also very empathic and sensed other people's emotions especially within my family. As I grew up I started to see Spirits, usually people who had passed over. Occasionally I would hear words or sentences and could smell scents'.

'When I was 5 I used to hear voices in my head which frightened me. I remember getting ready for primary school and there was a lady that used to slur my words and repeat them back to me in a negative way and flip words. I used to say to mum I can hear voices, she used to brush it off, but it got worse. I have now made my peace with it but it was hard when I was young'.

So potentially easier for Lisa and Leila to find their way to work with Spirit as they had had a range of experiences from a young age. For others having an enquiring and open mind led them to their first encounters. Despite a scientific view of the world and a negative view of Spiritualists themselves, Margaret decided she would at least try to confirm her suspicions.

> 'I didn't really know anything about Spiritualists so I went along (to a Spiritualist meeting). At that stage I thought Spiritual connection to people who have died was all a con. I'm a scientist so anything for which there isn't clear evidence is difficult for me to believe'.

However, observing a session, she was amazed by the accuracy of the Spiritualist describing events she could not possibly have known about.

> 'The Spiritualist running the session told me so many things that she couldn't possibly have known about me. Even allowing for the possibility of the Spiritualist being a good judge of character she just couldn't have known the things they (the Spirits) told me about people I knew who had passed on'.

Many interviewees described having had a life experience that left them feeling very low and desperate. Some were depressed and called out for help. This is where the Angels are listening and waiting to come forward and offer love and guidance. Roy described a moment where lots of events happened in close succession and he searched for help to make him feel more at ease.

> 'I was feeling pretty low, my Dad had just died, my wife had an accident and broken her elbows and so the prospect of spending two hours just being quiet with

someone who would help (a healer) seemed the right thing to do and I also thought it might do me some good'.

Mary, following a bereavement developed anorexia and found meditation helped her towards a better weight.

'My mother passed away when I was 23 from cancer and that was when my Spiritual path started, ... I was suffering from anorexia ... I was taught how to meditate and I had some acupuncture and Reiki... the treatment continued and I went from 6 stone to 8.5 stone in that time. The stress was causing the anorexia and I learned how I needed to love and look after my body to give me the fuel to keep going. It was extremely hard and a very difficult time in my life'.

For Rita it was a breakdown and depression that meant she called out for help and felt she was answered. Prior to this moment she had heard voices in her head but she ignored them. She was worried others might judge her harshly but at her lowest moment she felt she had been listened to by the Angels.

'I couldn't really tell anyone what these voices in my head were saying to me. If you tell people they think you are mad and I was frightened they would take my children away from me. I was scared lost and alone. I had a meltdown moment. I just gave in and said I can't do this anymore and I just said 'somebody help me!'. I then looked at my children and realised they needed me. I realised then that somebody must have been listening'.

In finding this help the interviewees were deeply affected by the instant solace that contact with Spiritualists offered. Whatever the route the general response was one of complete happiness and the certainty that they had found the help they felt they needed. Lauren attended a healing group. At first she was very nervous about what she would find and was concerned about entering a room full of strangers.

> 'All I can say is that I felt absolutely consumed with love for and from this group of women. I can't explain the type of love. I have love in my life from my family and my friends but this was something else. Something I'd never experienced. It was all consuming and non-judgemental and compassionate'.

When Lou finally asked for help she heard an inner voice comforting her and she knew she was not alone.

> 'I just kept going and listening to my inner voice, fanning the flame. At one point I was meditating and I stopped breathing. There was silence and I heard this strong voice saying 'We're here' and although I questioned what I was hearing I stayed with it and walked out of the marriage. It was like a razor blade coming from inside out but I did it and trusting the flame helped me'.

Martin was not prepared to even consider the potential for anything other than an earth life but once he had a diagnosis of cancer he decided to seek help from a Spiritual healer. He found that the healer provided an accurate diagnosis without being told and felt calm and at peace in the presence of Spirits he said:

> 'I am now open minded, I am still a sceptic but seeing is believing'.

The initial searching involved different routes for different people, young and older, male and female. Once found, choosing different ways to work with Spirit and become more aware of individual Guardian Angels, became a continual and often rewarding journey.

Finding ways to work with Spirit

Each of the interviewees described both how they found ways to work with Spirit and some described how the effects of their work manifested in their lives. For all it was a journey. The journey could be full of doubt and false starts but the overall effect of giving time and paying attention to the workings of their minds aided by their Guardian Angels, helped them to come to terms with their problems. Lauren describes some of her false starts.

> 'I wondered about whether the church would be important to me again. I looked at Alpha courses where I heard they talked about the meaning of life. It just didn't appeal to me. I work on the principle that if I don't make it happen it's because it isn't right. Now I think this is where the Angels came in and they sorted it'.

Once familiar with the concept of a Guardian Angel understanding their particular role and the help they could offer has been deeply comforting and helpful for many of those interviewed. Jennie has come to understand how her Guardian Angel can help.

'Your Guardian Angels are with you from the day you are born to the day you die and you just have to ask them for help. I did and it worked. For example, last year my daughter wanted me to do the London marathon with her. I wasn't sure but I said yes. Then my daughter was injured and I had to do it alone. I had a painful knee and I was not sure I'd make it. I asked my Guardian Angel to stay with me... the run was really hard but I did feel I was protected ... and I managed the whole distance with my Angel's help'.

Val has always felt comfortable talking to her Spirits. She has both auditory and visual experiences and has formed a good relationship with those she talks to:

'It's important to develop your third eye on your forehead to be able to see into the Spirit world. For me I don't see things, it's more like hearing from a third ear. It just pops into my head. I have three guides with me. If one of my Spirit guides is too close I get a bad headache. Another has a great sense of humour and always gives me as a first message the word cauliflower. He thinks this is highly amusing. I can hear him laughing because I've said cauliflower again'.

Following her divorce Lou needed a great deal of emotional help. She began by exploring crystals and meditating.

'I could feel something shifting. I might be curled up on the office floor crying feeling that I was tearing my children's life apart but a small part of me was saying your kids will be fine. I've read that the quietest voice within you is your higher self speaking to you. The next voice is your heart and the loudest is your head. I listened to that quiet voice and I attached to that. I have had so much judgment in my life. I felt then that I had a flame burning inside me and I had to pay attention to it'.

Rita talks about how finally acknowledging the voices in her head meant that she could begin to use them to help her manage the difficulties in her life. She developed a technique which finally helped her lift her mood.

'When I just asked for help it was like a presence came to me and started whispering and telling me what to do. I had been saying I don't feel well, I am not happy because the feeling in my body was that I didn't feel good. The whispering said "why don't you feel you are happy, say you're happy", so I started saying that all day long. Very quickly it all went away'.

Mary continued finding the help she needed and reaped the benefits of both healing and contacting those who had been lost to her during her life

'I felt his wonderful feeling of being surrounded by Angels, this immense warmth on my cheeks, I had some big releases, my legs were jerking, I visualised putting all the bad things I had been holding onto in my life into a golden hot air balloon and let them go. I felt my Mum and my grandmother with me which was so comforting but also knowing that there is more to life, there is a beyond and everything is ok when people die. We grieve so much when people die but they have an important job to do in heaven. I do believe my Mum and grandparents are looking after me and the girls which makes me feel strong'.

Despite her initial doubt as Margaret continued on her journey and worked more with a Spiritualist group she too began to receive messages from Spirit that she felt sure enough about to pass on to those for whom they were intended.

'I would sit quietly and concentrate on the thoughts in my head. All of a sudden ideas and thoughts where coming to me. I got good at passing on messages. I could hear a voice in my head telling me things about the people in the group. For example, I went up to someone in the class and said 'You have a twin, don't you? No one else in the class knew that this person had a twin who had died. I said it and I don't know where it came from. I kept going and thoroughly enjoyed it. It was all so interesting to watch as well as be part of'.

As our journey continues the firm belief that Guardian Angels are available to all of us supports our existence in this life. Working with Spirit creates the circumstances both to take care of ourselves because we feel loved and supported in everything we do and then to take care of others. As Eleanor describes:

'I believe that we all have a Spirit which is our life force and when we die our Spirit lives on. I believe that Angels are very special Spirits that God has chosen as his messengers to help and guide us on earth and, hopefully, when our time comes to pass on to the next life they will greet us and guide us on our new path'.

Rachel having always had some sense of the other realm decided to train as a Reiki Master and use her knowledge to help others.

'I have always had chats with God ever since I can remember and I really started following my Spiritual path when I completed my Reiki 1 and 2 courses and in particular, when I read 'A Little Light' by Diana Cooper – it's been by my bed ever since'.

Anne's view of the ways Angels work in her life has also deepened her understanding of her life with Spirit.

'My understanding is that there is a different vibrational energy within Spirit so different beings give off a different frequency and that is the only difference for me between Angels and Spirit'.

At 16 years old Jo's life working with Spirit and understanding the role of Guardian Angels has already begun. To have this help so early is a great gift as he will have this help as he makes decisions all his life. It takes some people many years to acquire this knowledge and understanding. Some only begin to understand at the end of their lives on earth.

'I do believe Angels are there for you and are looking down on you, you just need to ask for help sometimes, they help give me guidance when I have challenges to deal with or difficult situations. I definitely feel I am a positive person; my glass is always half full and I always look on the bright side of life. It's important to be able to live your life to the fullest'.

Guardian Angels appear to have different personalities and as familiarity with them deepens some people described their own relationship and how they work together. Rachel makes an attempt to describe this very special bond.

> 'My Guardian Angel is always very shy; I have never seen her but can feel her around me. I believe somebody is looking after me, a wonderful presence which is very comforting. I feel when I am meditating, I try and push out all the noise and fill the space with a soft white light and feel that is part of my aura and Guardian Angel. I can't describe it any better than that'.

As the work continues several interviewees tried to describe how they found the difference between the Spirit world and their Guardian Angel. This is important because some people consider anything they experience, at a deeper level than ordinary life, as the work of Spirit or Spirits (people who have passed on) and others are aware of a difference between Spirits and Angels (a higher order of beings who have not lived in this reality and act as guides and teachers). Ultimately it is more important to concentrate on the energy provided by deep experience and to recognise the unconditional love offered. It seems unnecessary to dwell too much on the difference but for those who want some clarity the following excerpts might help.

> 'I think a Spirit has been alive in this life in flesh and bone and some Spirits come back although I'm not sure why that is and some come back and touch you and you get a feeling in your head. Angels I visualise they are floaty, they are more powerful than Spirits and have the ability to heal and guide us with strong messages'.

Leila wonders whether the idea of Spirit is personal to each one of us.

> 'I think we all have a Spirit within us but only some of us have the power to take on other people's pain and help them. All the Angels have different powers and say we all need support down here. They want us to have self-love, healing and strength'.

Roy has a more pragmatic view and helpful to those who may find the concepts of Angels and Spirits more difficult.

> 'I just feel there has to be something more than this once we leave. We are made of energy and energy doesn't disappear just because someone has passed over. Energy can neither be created nor destroyed so it must go somewhere'.

Having found their way to Spirit and worked with other realities in their own way, the interviewees described how long-term familiarity and understanding had begun to create a different and enhanced way of seeing this world and their relationships with other people.

Other benefits

Some interviewees now looked for signs their Guardian Angels were around and keeping a watch over them. When problems occurred this was deeply comforting and reassuring. As Jennie says:

> 'I think I see more now. I am aware of presences and I see signs, for example feathers on the floor. I just know

the Angels are around. I've done a Reiki course, I've done Anusha healing and now I feel I have a Spiritual toolbox. I've given up alcohol. I eat healthily. I feel in control. I feel very fulfilled. I feel I'm on the right path'.

In times of difficulty Mary has received direct help from Spirit. She has both heard and felt their presence and found huge comfort in knowing she is not alone.

'I had an experience last year when a Spirit came to the house, I ignored it for a few weeks, it was black shadow standing and watching me from the corner of a room, I didn't feel frightened and just tried to ignore it. When I was working in the office from home one day, Spiritual music started playing which I thought I can't ignore this anymore, somehow thought it was like a protector then, that wanted me to know they were there to help'.

Lauren has found she is happier and more confident than ever before. This feeling was echoed by all the interviewees. It may be that just taking time for themselves and monitoring their emotions had a stabilising effect but importantly they felt that they were never alone and were unconditionally loved.

'I'm more confident and happier... I don't see anything I just feel things and I know my Guardian Angel is on my face. It's a knowing. I have conversations with the Angels. I know we are absolutely surrounded with the Angels who help us in our daily life if we ask them for help. Once you do and once you start realising how they are working in your life it's wonderful. I am so much more grateful for everything in my life. I think I'm a kinder person and much more open to others' stories and situations.

That doesn't mean that following a life in Spirit means that you believe without thought, consideration or judgement. A questioning approach is important and can lead to a deeper understanding of how we receive help. Lou is very aware she has a critical mind and monitors her responses to her life in Spirit. Ultimately, having tried a variety of routes, she feels connected to the Spirit world and receives the loving benefits of doing so.

'A lot of the time I doubt it and think I'm making it up but the more I do this work the more I am convinced about the need to listen to your inner voice...that Source is ultimately love. So often formalised religion is based on fear, it's a railway line that stops people thinking and feeling'.

Eleanor is also more confident and happier feeling she is not alone but has a being to turn to when she needs help.

'Believing in a Spiritual path has helped me because I know that my Guardian Angels are watching over me and I will never be alone'.

It does not seem to be just that the interviewees felt cared for and loved but it has also helped them consider mortality and face life difficulties. Lauren explains that it doesn't stop problems from occurring, that is part of life, but responding to them calmly, considering a course of action, helps to live a more peaceful existence.

'I believe we still have choice and I believe we still have freedoms but for all of us there is a date and a time we will die. I've done lots of growing about past experiences and even challenges now and I'm a lot calmer. When something is thrown at me, I think ok this has been sent to me for a reason so what are the reasons'.

Leila describes how the process of developing her awareness of how the Spirit world works in her life has helped her with her relationship with those she finds create difficult emotions in her.

'I feel it has helped enormously with consolation when I have challenging times and guides me when I'm not sure what to do. It has also helped me forgive when I have struggled with doing so'!

In some ways the process of sitting and listening to our inner thoughts or voices gives us the space to begin to manage those thoughts, to reject the negative ones and concentrate on the positive. Rita has managed to achieve this, despite the fact that she still has difficult times, she feels she knows what to do to help herself.

'We are all looking for something but all we have to do is listen to the best friend inside us. We all have the negative voice but when I work with people I say to give the negative bully voice a name and reject it. The nice voice, if you take the time to listen, will remind you to take your umbrella on a rainy day, it leads you to your goal. It talks to you when you are walking and meditating. It's there for you to guide you on your journey'.

And Jo has learned he will be able to use his knowledge throughout his life. Working with Spirit and identifying his

Guardian Angel who he talks to when life is challenging has really helped what for many young people can be a puzzling time.

> 'It has taught me the importance of self-worth and having the confidence to follow my passion. I feel incredibly lucky to have that at 16'!

For Mary the lessons learned from reaching out and asking for help have helped her reevaluate how she deals with problems that might occur in her life.

> I think everyone has their own journey and you have to experience the Spiritual side of life for yourself at the right time. You have to walk the walk before you can appreciate how special it is, I feel so honoured to be on this Spiritual path and feel truly blessed....'

> 'Believe in yourself and believe what's out there and that will change your life, you will never be alone with your Guardian Angel by your side. Whatever tragedy you have had whether mental or physical you just have to believe they have been brought to you for an opportunity to grow'.

Beth came to June for healing session and describes the experience of having a great weight removed from her which left her feeling uplifted and happy

> 'I went for a healing session and she started going down my right side of my body it was all beautiful and warm. I was visualising lying in the most vibrant meadow with warmth and comfort then she started coming up my left side and it all went dark, heavy,

cold - where's my happy place gone? Then she came up to the top of my chest and literally there was a big stone on my chest that turned and it uncoiled it was like a Gollum, that stared at me coming out of my chest then it just jumped off and scuttled off. Then June was at my head and I was back in my meadow! Then I realise my breathing was feeling better. It was an entity that was in me. From that day on my sense in my chest changed and I have been better ever since'.

Being someone who feels comfortable talking to their Guardian Angel can be demanding because many people will dispute the truth of the work done. There will always be doubters and learning how to manage differences is all part of the journey.

The critical voice

Most of the interviewees were aware they might be judged by others for their views. Some had a critical voice in their own heads wondering from where these thoughts and ideas were coming. The situation can only be positive because blind faith can lead to a belief that an individual is right and therefore others are wrong. Throughout history the fanatical adherence to a faith or way of life has often caused conflict and division. Understanding our thoughts and being prepared for discussion is all part of living in Spirit. As Rachel says:

'Believe what you believe, everyone has a choice, why would you dismiss something you haven't tried. I would

> encourage everyone to find their path to follow it's personal preference'.

Leila agrees and is willing to deal with doubters in a peaceful way.

> 'I don't worry at all if people think this is all nonsense. I feel 100% happy and committed to what I believe and so am happy to walk away'.

Anne feels the value of having been given an inner strength through her work in Spirit means she can feel strong enough to walk away when doubters challenge her.

> 'I don't mind if people have their own view. I don't feel I need to explain to anyone about how I feel. It feels like it is my own inner strength and I don't need anyone's approval, I think believing in myself and having self-worth, this has transformed my life'.

Margaret continues to question herself and finds the idea of Angels hard to comprehend. However, that doesn't mean the process of receiving messages from Spirits hasn't enhanced her life. There are many ways to work with the other realm and Margaret is a good example of developing skills that can help others.

> 'I have no idea where the messages come from whether it's just intuition I really don't know. I'm an atheist so find it hard to believe in Angels. I am aware of the ideas and messages coming into my head and then, when I pass them on they turn out to be true and have value for the person hearing them'.

There is a need for this rational and scientific approach to our relationship with Spirit. Its important to question and try to understand further why some people find the link easy to access and others reject or use it in different ways. As Margaret continues:

> 'I have thought a lot about the way we celebrate Christianity. I now think it's better for like-minded people to meet together without the restrictions of the church to explore alternate realities. My husband was a scientist and he believed we were all made from stardust but who knows. It's important to be sceptical. We need to ask how do people know things about the Spirits of people who are no longer with us and how do they have this new knowledge? From a scientific point of view, you can't kill energy so maybe some people are better able to pick up these energies than others'.

Carol knows people doubt the presence of a Spirit world but she feels sure that if they took the time to listen to their inner voice they too would meet their guides

> 'I smile and say its ok when people think this is all nonsense. I used to be where you are now, I used to think what you are thinking. Its good to be cynical to begin as we all have to start somewhere. You can only begin to believe when you start to experience something that you know you felt, saw what was as real to you with someone you trust, then little by little as your awareness grows you begin to 'know' what you experience is real. A good

> teacher helps you to find all this wonderful magic out for yourself in your own time'.

Lou is aware of all the gifts she has received by working with Spirit and considering how Spirit has worked in her life. She had been very distressed and now she feels able to deal with many of the conflicts that continue to turn up in her life. Without this support and unconditional love she feels life would be very lonely.

> 'Things tend to be about love or fear and maybe some scientists would prefer not to dwell on those two aspects of life because they are messy and so they focus only on those things to which they can find answers. It makes me feel sad because I think they lose so much of the flavour of life'.

Eleanor has felt able to challenge those who have disputed her beliefs. She has found meaning in her life though her relationship with her Guardian Angel and so values the positive effects of that relationship that to live without it seems to her a lesser life.

> 'Most people I know have some sort of belief and I accept that they must choose their own path. If someone really does not believe in Angels and Spirits I just ask them to explain what they think is the point of it all if there are no Angels to guide us and there is nothing after we die. No one has come up with a better explanation yet'.

Jo too realises there will be those who would have rejected a Spiritual path as unbelievable but that has not changed his own views.

'I appreciate not everybody is on the same Spiritual path but feel that I am a good, honest, kind person following a path on which I feel really comfortable. It gives me a lot of fulfilment and happiness'.

Many of the interviewees talked about how they manage the discussions with people who aren't interested in Spirit. Rita described how she translates her own beliefs for her children. Her intention is to prepare them for a way to manage the problems they might encounter in their lives.

'Generally, I attract fellow mediums or people who are in contact with the Spirit world, but I am aware it can be taken the wrong way and I'm careful not to bring it up if I meet a new person until they do. When I talk to the children I explain some of the things that go wrong in their lives by saying you are on your road and it's a good straight road but sometimes there are little bumps but you will get over them. You may make a decision to take another path but ultimately the guides will guide you back to the path you should have been on'.

Even knowing that some people think 'it's a load of rubbish' Jennie has recognised the need to keep an open heart and that this state of being open to others, to being open to new ideas and to being open to the power of the universe to change the way we feel about ourselves and others is a truer way of living that narrowing a focus to this reality only.

'I know some people think all this is a load of rubbish but I think this is all about having an open heart and being open to question and to make up your own mind. Of course, if you sit quietly for two hours you are bound to feel a bit better because you have taken time out of your day to rest. But anything is better than nothing, everyone takes it at a different level. I think it's important to let everyone find their own way. For me it has opened my heart and helped me on my way and I hope I can help other people now'.

And for Martin who was so sceptical he finished his interview by saying.....

'Anyone that thinks this is a lot of nonsense I would have agreed but as a last resort you have nothing to lose it can only help and be open minded'.

Opening the heart

Ultimately all the interviewees felt that in opening their hearts to the possibility of Angels and Spirit they had found a way of living that was both enhanced in experience and full of love. They had chosen their path and were willing to accept that it might not be for everyone. They had questioned their new knowledge and understanding, their new relationship with their Guardian Angel and found love and support. The following comments echo Stuart's

'We need to surround ourselves with light, to imagine ourselves protected from harm and to trust in the Angels' support'.

'I now know if you create a space in your life to listen to your inner voice you will be given help and guided.

Ultimately though, you make your own decisions maybe based on the guidance your inner voice has offered, but not in a dictatorial way... .....the confidence to stay in a connected space, to desire that connected space, to trust it. What was 14 years ago a little flame now it's a lantern with glass around it and it's here to stay'.

'My response now would be don't judge, go out there and try to explore the alternative treatment, healing can and does help. Try to understand the work Spiritualists do and try it for yourself. I think there would be a lot of surprised people as I was'.

I'm also more comfortable about life and death now too. I am not afraid of dying. I am just so appreciative of the life I have now. I am a much happier person'.

Mary's feeling is why not open your hearts. It won't harm you and you may receive the love you have been looking for.

'Believe in yourself and believe what's out there and that will change your life, you will never be alone with your Guardian Angel by your side. Whatever tragedy you have had whether mental or physical you just have to believe they have been brought to you for an opportunity to grow'.

David has found that developing a Spiritual path has helped him to relax more, to not get so anxious and to be happier,

'I feel very much aware now of Spirituality, through doing meditation and healing in my later years, it helps me immensely. I have always got really angry and very much a control freak. This has taught me not to judge people, they may be doing things the way they think is right, the way they have been taught but not necessarily the way I think. It has helped me understand, accept things, enjoy more and I am a much happier person now. Like most people I have had challenging times this has helped me put this behind me and move forward. I have been working hard on releasing past traumas and this is definitely work in progress but I am getting there'.

Rita talked about the relief at feeling listened to and the importance of self-forgiveness,

'You are being listened to, you are being heard, released to be free who you want to be. Be on your path, we always carry lots of baggage from our childhood. It's as though it was embedded and needed to be released, we have to forgive ourselves and this is one of most powerful stories I share with my clients'.

Carol explains how working with Spirit has changed her life and made her appreciate herself and her place in the world

'This has completely changed my life and myself, allowing me to be a truer version of myself after releasing lots of patterns, clearing traumas, past life issues, karma. I know I am surrounded by the Universe and its beings of Light, helping me on my journey. Helping me to see the magic in the world, in nature, in people, in synchronicities, to be able to experience fully how amazing the world is, and beyond. It has helped me to help others. Mainly it has helped me to be happy within myself, and now I am a unique being experiencing all that I can, and I am loved by all the higher realms'.

Rita talks about the need to forgive others who may have hurt you and ultimately to forgive yourself. Following a break with her husband he became very ill.

'On this Saturday morning I had this strong message to say you need to forgive him I sat on the floor in my kitchen and this power came over me. It was so strong, something like I had never experienced before, I sat there on my knees and said I really forgive you, this is the power of forgiveness with all of my whole heart, I forgive you Nick you can go home now, five minutes later I got the call to say he had passed'.

For Beth working in the Spiritual realm has helped her live a fuller and more appreciative life. She says,

'I feel Angels are with you all the time, you have your own Guardian Angel .. to ask when you need help. Spirits are there to guide you and Angels are there to protect and communicate with you...'

Stuart feels that unless we open our hearts to Spirit, we will stay caught in the everyday struggles that life throws at us. He is so insistent that there is more than this life and it is there for us to be enjoyed. It is there for us to feel loved and it is there for us to find our way. As Stuart said 'Let's *get this show on the road!'.* It's time to start your journey'.

June and Stuart hope you will find this book helpful and useful. If it brings comfort and answers some of your life questions, then its presence in the world will be a success.

A final word from Stuart

We asked Stuart to say some final words. June spent time listening quietly. She sat in her sunny room surrounded by light and looked content. Then Stuart started to talk ...

'It's very important for people to realise when they really do fall down and beg for help, that there is always help there. They need to know where they go to help, they need to know there are people to help and support them. They have to realise it's not a weakness to ask for help or fall down or feel unworthy or unloved, it's just finding a path for them to be supported and helped. There is no weakness in asking.

I know I was worried about asking for help and I didn't and it led to me taking my own life. I hope this book helps people to find a path, to find people to help both in the non-Angel world and with me. If you avoid a problem it just keeps coming back in different ways until you sort it out. Not everyone can find a path to peace immediately but humanity can call on us, we are here to help and to listen. We are always listening.

Sadness overcomes people. We see it as a black cloud. Don't wait until you are desperate to ask for help, talk to us often and *connect to a higher voice. Connect to your own voice in the Spirit world.*

Taking time to listen to your inner voice is important. Taking time to be peaceful. Listening first to the many beautiful sounds of the world, the birdsong, the wind in the leaves and then moving to your inner voice. I am concerned that the human race doesn't take time to listen to each other. Once you are aware of your own inner voice, listening to others will create a greater connection, an empathy.

Sometimes people smile but they might be hurting inside and maybe only their Spirit guide or Spirit helpers can help them. If we the Spirit world could teach people to talk to us may be saying.

Sadness is a sickness and it builds up and then people become physically ill. I just want to help people avoid that sadness, by seeing nature in its beauty and to hear birds sing and smell the flowers. Humanity seems to have forgotten how wonderful the planet is. Let us help you to remember.

We speak of love and you speak of love but it gets muddled with romantic love. Real love from us will make your heart sing. I hope we can help people with the book here and from the words we have spoken

So I ask you to help me to communicate through this book. We all come from the same essence and once we know this and know we are interconnected there will be peace'.

EPILOGUE

We would also like to share with you another message from Katy Gostick as June asked her to channel a message from a Rose in her garden, where she saw Stuart standing one day whilst being interviewed for the book.

Katy says that "June gave me this beautiful delicate rose and asked me if I could get a message from her, and I think my first words were 'she's bringing in the Divine Feminine energy'...

The Angels of the Divine Feminine

The Rose told me that she was the Angelic Ray of the Divine Feminine energy. I believe that the angels connected with this rose are somehow bringing us a finer, lighter vibration of the Divine Feminine which perhaps is easier for us to feel and bring into our denser human bodies. I wonder if this is useful for those of us touched by grief from the loss of children or other difficult traumas that close our heart centres.

Our ability to love, to feel loved and to love ourselves fully is compromised by deep trauma and this beautiful rose is asking us to breathe her essence and energy into our hearts and allow the pale pink vibration of love to help repair our broken hearts and bring healing for our soul. Allowing you feel to more balanced, calm and at peace.

This rose is called 'New Dawn' and she is guiding us towards the New Golden Age here on planet Earth. Our transition into this New Age is not without some difficult challenges, and the energy from this rose is gifted to us from the angels to help our journey.

June is also a gift from God, a being of light, who can help transmute divine angelic love from Source ⚘

ACKNOWLEDGEMENTS

I would like to acknowledge and say a special Thank You to all these wonderful talented people that came together to make this book a reality.

Jane Grose and Jac Wallace who offered to write this book, who gave up their precious time to make this happen. To give Spirit a voice and to help humanity from a caring, loving place.

Stuart Barclay my beautiful son, who is in Spirit, helped to keep us all motivated and channeled lots of the content of the book.

To all those wonderful people that gave up their time to do the interviews. This helped so much as it's in their words the way spirit has helped in their lives.

To Sarka Darton and Katie Tythridge for the wonderful art work.

To Marilu Wren who believed the concept of what we were all trying to achieve with this book. She took on the task of formatting and publishing and actually making this book a reality.

Last but not least my wonderful husband Charlie, who has welcomed these friends into our home, made lunch and endless cups of tea so the work on the book could actually happen. For being so understanding to how important my work with Spirit is.

GLOSSARY

Dowsing with a pendulum – this is a technique to connect with the angels and ask questions.

Guardian Angel is an angel that is assigned to protect and guide you throughout your life, from the moment you are born until the day you die. Exclusively yours and are like a nurturing mother with unconditional love. Guardian angels can give comfort, offer guidance and bring people and opportunities into your life.

Archangels are the highest rank of Angels and provide the highest good, they come to us with love, acceptance, understanding and compassion. There are 15 archangels and are described below:-

Archangel Ariel – Lioness of God is an archangel of nature, healing, spiritual development. She is known for being the Guardian and healer of animals. Her energy is powerful but gentle. She inspires growth and encourages people to live to their full potential.

Archangel Azrael- Whom God Helps he is described as the Angel of Death but in a good way. He comforts families and friends whose loved one passed and offers compassion and wisdom. He is here to remind us that we have much to live for even after death.

Archangel Chamuel- He who sees God is an archangel of bravery, courage, and justifiable anger, helps find lost objects. He is also known for helping us raise our intuition and vibrations, helping us receive or channel messages.

Archangel Gabriel – Strength of God is the archangel of dreams, messages, joy, light, peace, hope, guidance and revelation. She is known as the communicator of God, her energy is uplifting and you can call upon her when you need help understanding, accepting and passing messages.

Archangel Haniel – Grace of God is an archangel with attributes of love, relationships, growth, healing, communication and protection. She is known for guiding those who seek to develop their physic abilities, spiritual talents and healing arts. You can call upon her when you need help expanding your intuition and psychic abilities.

Archangel Jeremiel – Mercy of God is described as the Angel of Hope, he is one of the Archangels who help people pass over to the spiritual realm. He helps souls review their life on earth and helps people learn from their mistakes. You can call upon him if you need help understanding where you went wrong or what you can do to resolve a situation.

Archangel Jophiel – Beauty of God she helps us when we feel the most insecure. She provides and instils beauty in our souls, she inspires people to search deep within themselves, helping us gain the confidence we need to feel and express beauty from the heart. She can also help us see the beauty in others and in our environment, helping us to appreciate and be grateful for what we have.

Archangel Metatron – Highest of Angels (twin) is the archangel of prayer and wisdom. He helps with those who are stressed or those who need focus, motivation, discipline and organisation in their lives. He's also known to help those who are starting a new project and need help with management. He represents the divine spark of God within us and is also known as the heavenly scribe. Considered the king of the angels, Metratron had an earthly existence as the prophet Enoch. He is the Guardian of the Guardian angels and the tallest angel in heaven.

Archangel Michael – He Who is Like God is the chief of the archangels and has great strength, power and courage. He helps with our life's purpose and his gifts to us are communication, problem-solving, sleep, strength, and letting the past go. He takes away negativity and fear.

Archangel Raguel – Friend of God is the angel of justice, he helps us with truth and honesty in ourselves and others. He is the mediator in challenging situations, especially if we have problems with another person. He helps us restore balance and peace.

Archangel Raphael – God Heals he helps with inner and outer healing (mental, emotional, physical, spiritual) and helps promote better health and spirituality. He is often known to assist those who heal others especially doctors and nurses.

Archangel Raziel – Secrets of God always knows the answers and is known as the most knowledgeable of all the angels. He has a deeper understanding of life in general and encourages us to strengthen our bonds to the spiritual realm.

Archangel Sandalphon - Highest of Angels (twin) One of the two twins who were once human but ascended into Angels. The twin of Metatron is known for delivering to God and represents our connection to both earth and heaven. He is the energy link between man and spirit, so his energy is swift and powerful.

Archangel Uriel – Light of God and is the leader of the angels of light, who illuminate truth and help the earth. He can help you find your life path, and is an angel of peace. Uriel helps us to achieve our higher self(mentally, emotionally and spiritually).

Archangel Zadkiel – Righteousness of God he helps with forgiveness and encourages us to have love for ourselves and to love others. He gives us strength to confront our wounds and he also reminds us to be grateful and appreciate the love we have in our lives.

Ascended Masters – are understood to be individuals who have lived in physical bodies, acquired the Wisdom and Mastery needed to become Immortal and free of the cycles of re-embodiment and karma, and have attained their "Ascension" (the sixth initiation).

Angel – is a messenger of God, characterised as having human form with wings and a halo, here to protect and guide human beings.

Scrying – is known as foretelling the future using a crystal ball.

Psychic Healing – this is an exchange of energy, it's like a conversation that takes place between two people's energies. Psychic healing involves one individual transferring healing energy to someone who needs it and the other person receiving that healing energy.

137

Affirmations – are positive statements that can help you to challenge and overcome self-sabotaging and negative thoughts. When you repeat them often, and believe in them, you can start to make positive changes. Affirmations strengthen us by helping us believe in the potential of an action we desire to manifest.

REFERENCE BOOKS

Baer R., Lykins, E., Peters J (2012)
Mindfulness and self-compassion as predictors of psychological wellbeing in long-term meditators and matched non-meditators. P p230-238. (https://doi.org/10.1080/17439760.2012.674548)

RECOMMENDED READING

Cooper D
'A Little Light on Spiritual Laws' Mobius; New Ed Edition 2004

Heartsong C
'Anna, Grandmother of Jesus, A Message of Wisdom & Love'

Frazier K
'Crystals for Beginners: The Guide to Get Started with the Healing Power of Crystals'

Cloud E
'Codependency No More: How to Cure Codependency, Start to Love Yourself and Fight for No More Codependent Relationship Ever'

YOUTUBE

We recommend that you listen to June's Podcasts where she shares further about her life to date and also some wonderful channeled insights from Spirit. https://bit.ly/3ztuNdd

June's Love Mediation has been recorded and is available at: https://youtu.be/Blk3mxC2S6Q

CONTRIBUTORS

Marilu Wren is an Energy Practitioner who is passionate about supporting and empowering women through holistic education and vibrational healing, so that they can connect to their inner voice, maintain their health, vitality and confidence. Please visit www.heraholistic.co.uk for more information.

Katy Gostick is a Spiritual Facilitator and she assists you to find peace, regain your inner balance and follow your dreams. Please visit www.katygostick.co.uk for more information.

JUNE IS AVAILABLE FOR:

Healing   – either over the phone or in person

Oracle Card readings   – via zoom or in person

Meditation Group   - The Temple Path is a wonderful collection of heart centred women who support each other's spiritual growth through weekly meditations and healing work.

Sisterhood Circle   - June helps to facilitate a monthly Sisterhood circle locally.

Retreats/Workshops   - June participates in regular spiritual/healing Retreats and Workshops both online and in person. Please see her website for more details.

If you would like to access healing from June please email her on june.barclay@hotmail.com and she will be happy to guide you on your journey.

For more information please visit her website at: www.junebarclay.co.uk.

TESTIMONIALS

TESTIMONIALS FOR JUNE'S MEDITATION WORK

Thank you to June and Marilu for the wonderful community of the Temple Path, to find this amazing spiritual group full of love, compassion , sincerity, support has come at the perfect time for me. Would recommend highly.   *Jacqui*

"If, like me, you have the inclination and hungry curiosity to explore and learn more about the energetic nature of your human being-ness, then you may find, as I have, that June's spiritually guided online Temple Path healing mediations can offer you a space where it is still possible to cultivate a conscious and real sense of connection with yourself and others, a much needed medicine in these disorientating and dismantling times.

Something magical happens when like hearted people get together. The space offered by those who bring the Temple Path to life provides each participant a quality of listening rarely found these days. A type of listening where anything can be said and heard, without judgment or any attempt to advise or council. A listening where the unseen becomes visible, the impossible, possible, the imaginable, real.

The support and grounded commitment available through The Temple Path mediations enabled a fear of speaking from my heart to dissolve and provided the ground on which I claimed my Sovereignty and my true voice." **Bronwyn**

I have known June for about 6 years and I have been very blessed to have experienced her powerful meditations in her healing hut. We are now at this moment in time having to adapt and the Temple path has given me the opportunity to still progress on my spiritual path.

The meditations on zoom are just as powerful and it is wonderful meeting new like-minded people through the group. It is a group for anyone no matter where you are on your spiritual journey. It is a place where you can feel safe and feel truly loved. **Bridget**

'Knowing I am part of a wonderful collective of like-minded others has been comforting, especially during these difficult times during lockdown. To share among us has been a real blessing to have somewhere to go and something to look forward to on Thursday evenings as well as added extras during the week. June of course is warm, welcoming and cares deeply for every one of us. Junes healing comes through in a deep way of which has saved me on many occasions, always appearing when I needed her most. Marilu has been a rock to create such a platform for all of us to meet and so, I thank both ladies and spirit for changing my life for the better, I'm not sure I could have done it without them.' **Jooli**

I feel in such good hands with June, safe, cosy and supported.

143

Such a lovely group. June is so easy to talk to and her guidance is really appreciated and gives me something to ponder on

June's angel healings and meditations feel like a very warm, soothing, familiar hug. No matter how I am feeling, I deeply relax when working with June and find I am taken away from myself and my body into a beautiful feeling of expanse and calm. When I come out of a healing or meditation, I feel a strong sense of peace and deep nourishment. I know that I have received the healing that I needed at that time and I sense that the angels were with me. So powerful.

I have found since doing the mediations regularly with June , that I go much deeper and that my body receives healing that often shows itself the following day. The work that is done with the Angelic Realm is profound.   ***Anon***

'June's incredibly deep, healing gift brings with it a lifetime's commitment and connection to spirit. I have personally felt the impact of her interactions physically and viscerally, and the guidance she receives has resonated emotionally every time.' ***Nikki***

"The meditation evenings with Temple Path and June are a lovely way to relax and take time for yourself, it gives you a feeling of absolute calmness."   ***Rachel***

TESTIMONIALS FOR JUNE'S HEALING WORK

I find difficult to express in words how incredibly gifted June is. She is kind, warm, sensitive, thoughtful and generous, with the most profound understanding for others. Also, we have not known each other for long and have never met in person, our few conversations were so far only conducted over Zoom or phone, she seem to very quickly gauge my needs. On one occasion, when we were just chatting, she has out of the blue offered me her help in a way of a distant healing. I accepted her offer. Coming from a traditional scientific background, this was my first.

Again, words will not adequately describe what have followed. Not only did I feel energetic influences, I have also experienced images of healing powers. The moment was completely transformative.

The back pain I was suffering from has disappeared, I had the best sleep for a long time and out of sudden, things in a physical world started to manifest and fall in place. I could not thank June enough. She has improved and enriched my life beyond any imagination. Thank you June for your care and kindness and for the most amazing experience. *Sarka*

"So far, I have been lucky enough to have two healing sessions with June over the phone. It's hard to explain something so strong and deeply felt and when you're in the middle of the session you are almost not there at all. I felt physical sensations, some really strong and sudden, but I felt calm and safe and like there was a team of people supporting me. After both healings I slept like a brick. The next day after both I still felt deeply relaxed and lighter at the same time. My symptoms had changed too.

I am so very grateful for this life changing experience. I work in energy healing too but had never experienced anything like this.

If you need healing on any level, don't hesitate, June has an incredible and powerful gift. "   *Jo*

I have had distance healing with June recently and it was a truly remarkable experience. I was laying down and I could feel the healing taking place and moving in waves up and down my body. The sensations and heat were intense but calming. I had such a deep and restful sleep that night and felt more at peace afterwards. June has a truly amazing gift.   ***Bridget***

"June gave me lovely distant Anusha healing. As soon as the healing started I could feel my left shoulder, arm and leg being firmly held still. I could also feel fingers holding the toes on my left foot. My throat felt like it was being closed and it was difficult to breathe but I didn't feel uncomfortable. It felt like energy was being pulled up through my throat. I could see blue sparkling orbs on my right side and then there was an intense heat from my waist up. There was then a pressure across the top of my head and my fore head. June explained that when the session was finished the healers would carry on giving me

146

healing. I felt really emotional later, an emotional release. Just what I needed. I feel so much better and uplifted. Lovely healing, so gentle but powerful. Thoroughly recommend June Barclay and her Anusha healing, thank you." ***Donna***

I asked June to help my 11 year old daughter who had experience a very intense dream the night before, siting a girl who looked haunted. When my daughter was with June and explaining the dream, June said she could see the girl next to Daisy and described her as my daughter had, with long black hair and eyes that were white. She took her to the healing hut where she laid Selenite crystals around her and started her work in helping the girl leave Daisy's body and go home to the light. Daisy described later that day how she felt her body (energetically) curve towards June and tilt downwards. As June helped the girl to go "home" she was aware of the intense sadness she felt. June explained that the girl was drawn to my daughters light and that she knew that she would be visiting June who would help her go home. It was an incredible experience for everyone involved. ***Marilu & Daisy***

After joining the wonderful meditation group The Temple Path, I asked June for an Angel Healing session as there was a lot of stress in my life and my body was breaking out in a variety of ailments. I've had remote healing before from different spiritual practitioners and so was expecting a similar experience eg: no real benefits to my conscious or physical self. I can honestly say that this particular session was incredibly calming and I genuinely felt a slight shift in my energy levels afterwards. As subtle as it was, it was noticeable and I felt more energised and less anxious. I am definitely going to have more healing with June, not only is she fantastic at making one feel completely comfortable, she possesses a 'true and very real' gift for working with spirit. **Jo**

Once again I entered into June's 'shed' and felt the sense of peace. It felt like the next chapter to my healing journey as we pulled some cards to give the signposts and direction. As I lay on the bed and started to relax Mother Teresa was present plus many other spiritual Beings. I felt so much going on in between drifting into a deep place of peace, I could feel that work was being done on me where I have suffered with physical pain and it was confirmed that a spirit doctor was working on me. The power of the session was so apparent as I came to get off the bed. A cup of tea was greatly appreciated to ground me! Since the session I have been very aware of the guidance that is coming through to keep me on the necessary path to resource myself to help me when my sensitivity and nervous system is being greatly challenged. This is really helping me to recover from a very long period in my life of ill health and struggle to stay grounded and learning to put my needs first to enable me to be fully present for others rather than be completely drained and then to collapse. Thank you June for all that you do!!! *Fleur*

"June provides a safe environment for her healing sessions. She puts you at ease as soon as you meet her and a sense of calmness takes over".   ***Rachel***

TESTIMONIALS FOR JUNE'S ORACLE CARD READINGS

Over the years I've had many tarot card readings and wanted to try an Oracle Card reading with June to see what it was like. I chose June for this as my healing experience with her was so amazing and was curious to see what would come up with the Angels - particularly as I was in the middle of trying to make a life changing decision and wanted some clarity on this choice I had to make. I was stunned at the cards that were pulled - they were so accurate and specific and related purely to my situation. It was also a 'gentle' reading without any negativity, but there was certainly advice that I knew I had to take to improve my mental approach towards life. But most importantly, it made my life-changing decision easy for me - I took it and I am now on a different path in life which I feel is the right one. Thank you June
Joanne

June has a friendly, fun personality that shines through her oracle card readings. Her readings are insightful and inspirational. June leaves you feeling empowered with the accurate guidance and support that her readings offer. I thoroughly recommend an oracle card reading with June.
Donna

A Life with Spirit